AN INTRODUCTION TO READING INSTRUCTION

Arne Sippola, Ph.D.
Eastern Washington University

KENDALL/HUNT PUBLISHING COMPANY
4050 Westmark Drive   Dubuque, Iowa 52002

Cover clipart from Macromedia Freehand Clipart.

Contents

CHAPTER ONE

DEFINITIONS OF READING

Definitions of Reading

Frank Smith:
"The reduction of uncertainty."

Eleanor Gibson &
Harry Levin:
"Reading is developing meaning from patterns of symbols which one recognizes and endows with meaning.

Roach Van Allen:
"Reading is developing meaning from patterns of symbols which one recognizes and endows with meaning."

Kenneth S. Goodman:
"Reading is a complex process by which a reader reconstructs, to some degree, a message encoded by a writer in graphic language."

Robert Ruddell:
"Reading is a complex psycholinguistic behavior which consists of decoding written language units, processing the resulting language counterparts through structural and semantic dimensions, and interpreting the deep structure data relative to an individual's established objectives."

John Carroll:
"We can define reading ultimately as the activity of reconstructing a reasonable spoken message from a printed text and making meaningful responses to the reconstructed message that would parallel those that would be made to the spoken message."

Rudolph Flesch:
"Reading means getting meaning from certain combinations of letters. Teach the child what each letter stands for and he can read."

William S. Gray:
"...the reader not only recognizes the essential facts or ideas presented, but also reflects on their significance, evaluates them critically, discovers relationships between them, and clarifies his understanding of the ideas apprehended."

Arthur Gates:
"Reading is not a simple mechanical skill; nor is it a narrow scholastic tool. Properly cultivated, it is essentially a thoughtful process. However, to say that reading is a 'thought-getting' process is to give it too restricted a description. It should be developed as a complex organization of patterns of higher mental processes. It can and should embrace all types of thinking, evaluating, judging, imagining, reasoning, and problem-solving. Indeed, it is believed that reading is one of the best media for cultivating many techniques of thinking and imagining."

D.W. Reed:
"Reading is the identification of linguistic forms from strings of written configurations that represent them, as evidenced by producing the conventional signs for the same linguistic forms in some other system of representation."

M. Robeck &
R. Wallace:
"Reading is a process of translating signs and symbols into meanings and incorporating the new information into existing cognitive and affective structures."

State of Michigan: "Reading is the process of constructing meaning through the dynamic interaction among the reader, the test, and the context of the reading situation."

Implications of the Michigan Definition

1. The reader's existing knowledge and interest affect what he or she is willing and able to read. For example, a remedial reader may be able to read sports material on the sixth grade level, but may be limited to a third grade level in a social studies text.

2. The text, or written language, is the information presented to the reader. The clarity and organization of the text will affect the reader's ability to make sense of it.

3. The context of the reading situation also affects the reading process. Some children find texts so frightening that they will have difficulty reading them. However, these children would be able to read the same material in a less threatening situation. The purpose or task of reading is also part of the reading situation. People read one way when trying to understand detailed directions and another when reading a novel for enjoyment. (I personally read with fear when presented with instructions of how to put a child's toy together!)

All of this adds up to: A person does not have one single reading level! Rather, background knowledge, interest, and the nature of the reading situation affect the level of the material he or she can read.

CHAPTER TWO

THEORETICAL MODELS OF READING

Perspectives of Reading

Although a comprehensive model of the reading process does not exist, reading authorities have given considerable attention to three conceptualizations of reading. These views are called top-down (or reader based), bottom-up (or text based), and interactive. All three share two similarities: (1) a reader and (2) a written text to read. The differences in perspective are based on the contributions of the readers as they read. The name of each view should help you remember its characteristics.

The Top-Down View

Those who consider reading to be a top-down (or reader-based) process focus on the reader. Readers do not begin reading with a blank mind; they bring knowledge based on past experiences with language and the world. In this view, fluent readers bring more information to the written text than the text itself provides. Because of this, they do not give close attention to words. Instead, they use their past experiences to predict meaning as they read. This predicting is also referred to as hypothesis testing, that is, sampling the text to test assumptions.

The top-down view emphasizes the reader and the reader's prior knowledge. For example, knowing that pepperoni is often a popular ingredient on pizzas is more important in reading "Sam ordered a pizza with olives, mushroom, and p_____" than knowing the sounds represented by the letter patterns in the word *pepperoni*. The top-down view suggests that the reader would predict *pepperoni* and use the text only for confirmation.

The Bottom-Up View

Another view of what happens during reading is bottom-up (or text based). In this view, the essential element in reading is the written text rather than what the reader brings. That is, the reader processes the text without much prior information about the meaning or content. Words and word parts are processed in order, and meaning is gleaned from this processing. In the example "Sam ordered a pizza with olives, mushrooms, and p_____," the bottom-up view holds that a reader would translate the word *pepperoni* into its oral language representation, assign meaning to it, and comprehend the meaning of the sentence.

The Interactive View

The third conceptualization is that reading is an interactive process. This combines the top-down and bottom-up views. In this view, fluent readers use both text features and background to understand written language (1).

Associated with the interactive view of reading is schema theory. Schema theory recognizes that reading involves many levels of analysis at the same time but at different levels. Levels include both text features (for example, letters, word order, and word meaning) and the reader's background knowledge (for example, content and hypotheses about meaning) (1). As readers process print, they construct meaning for segments of it based on both the print and background knowledge. For example, in reading about how to grow vegetables, readers integrate knowledge about gardening and related experiences with new information. They process the text to formulate hypotheses that make sense in light of existing background knowledge.

From *Principles and Practices of Teaching Reading*, 7/E by Heilman et al, © 1990. Reprinted by permission of Prentice-Hall, Inc., Upper Saddle River, NJ.

A Sample Bottom-Up Model of Reading:
One Second of Reading

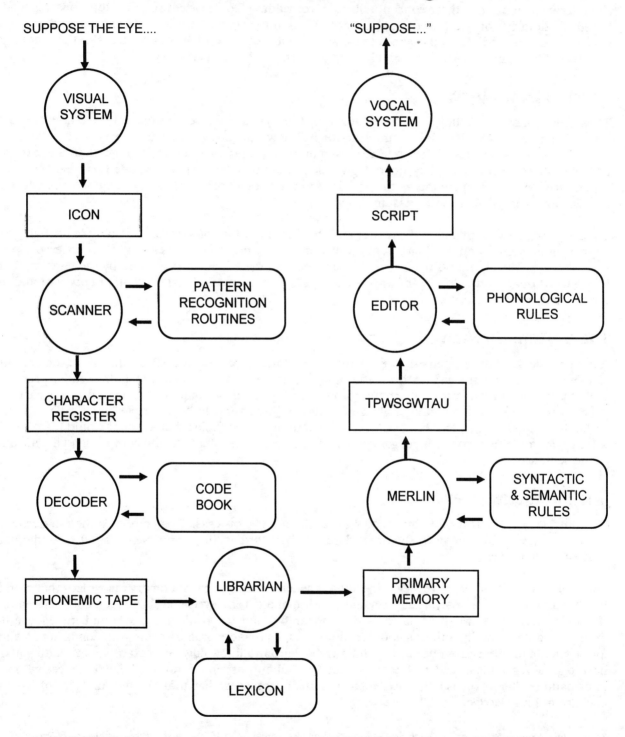

Source: Gough, P. (1985). One second of reading. In H. Singer and R. Ruddell (Eds.), *Theoretical Models and Processes of Reading* (pp. 661–686). Newark: International Reading Association.

Description of Gough's Model of Reading

1. Visual System

    A. Eye fixation (250 msec.)
    B. Eye sweeps 10-12 letter spaces to the right (saccadic eye movement) consuming 10-23 msec.
    C. A visual pattern is reflected onto the retina.
    D. An icon is formed.

2. Icon

    A. A relatively direct representation of a visual stimulus that persists for a brief period after the stimulus vanishes: Suppose
    B. The icon lasts for less than 1/2 second in light.

3. Scanner

    A. uses:

4. Pattern Recognition Routines

    A. Analyzing the lines, curves, and angles of the icon recognizing them as familiar patterns—letters of the alphabet—as indicated in his/her:

5. Character Register

    A. The letter or group of letters is/are presented to the system's:

6. Decoder

    A. The Decoder uses the reader's available:

7. Code Book

    A. To translate graphemes into phonemes which are, in word form, presented to the system's:

8. Librarian via

9. Phonemic Tape

    A. The Librarian refers to the reader's:

10. Lexicon

    A. Where the words are assigned meaning.
    B. The words (perhaps 4 or 5) and assumed meanings are briefly stored in the reader's:

---

11. Primary Memory and presented to:

12. MERLIN

    A. Merlin tries to discover the deep structure through the grammatical relationships among the words.

    B. If Merlin is successful, a semantic interpretation of the fragment is achieved and placed in the "ultimate register":

13. TPWSGWTAU (The Place Where Sentences Go When They Are Understood)

    A. The sentences are presented to the:

14. Editor

    A. Who, consulting the reader's:

15. Phonological Rules

    A. And constructs a:

16. Script

    A. Which is presented to the reader's

17. Vocal System

    A. Producing, one second after reading begins, the first word: "Suppose."

A "Top-Down" Perspective

Reading According to Frank Smith

1. Visual Information

   A. Print

2. Non-visual Information

   A. Syntactic Information
   B. Semantic Information
   C. "Theory of the World in the Head"

Fluent Reading

Fluent readers are less dependent upon visual information and tend to sample text to confirm or disconfirm their predictions.

Non-fluent Reading

A. Tunnel Vision: The inability to predict coming meanings due to an overload of visual information. Beginning and remedial readers often find themselves with this phenomenon.
B. Causes of Tunnel Vision:

   1. Trying to read something that is nonsense.
   2. Lack of relevant knowledge.
   3. Reluctance to use non-visual information.
   4. Poor reading habits (slowness; word-by-word reading; "sounding-out"; fear to predict).

Frank Smith on Comprehension

"The basis of comprehension is prediction and prediction is achieved by making use of what we already know about the world,...by making use of the theory of the world in the head."

A "Top-Down" Paradigm

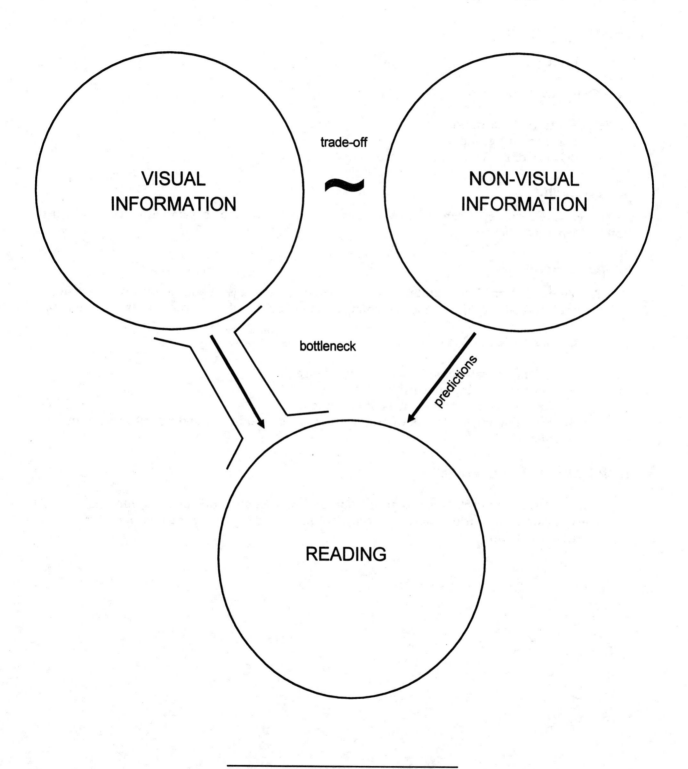

Interactive Model of Reading

A reader uses top-down and/or bottom-up strategies depending upon the complexity of the material in relation to an individual's schema(ta) for the topic at hand.

An Example of Top-Down Reading

"What a lot of hairy-faced men there are around nowadays. When a man grows hair all over his face it is impossible to tell what he really looks like. Perhaps that's why he does. He'd rather you didn't know. Then there's the problem of washing. When the very hairy ones wash their faces, it must be as big a job as when you and I wash the hair on our heads." (from The Twits, by R. Dahl)

An Example of Bottom-Up Reading

"We have shown that whenever we have k groups of n observations each, it is always possible to analyze the total sum of squares into two parts: the within treatment sum of squares and the treatment sum of squares. The degrees of freedom associated with the total sum of squares will be kn-1. The within treatment sum of squares will have k(n-1) d.f. and the treatment sum of squares will have k-1 d.f. (from Experimental Design in Psychological Research, Edwards)

Transactional Psycholinguistic Model

"Texts are constructed by authors to be comprehended by readers. The meaning is in the author and the reader. The text has a potential to evoke meaning but has no meaning in itself. How well the writer constructs the text and how well the reader reconstructs it and constructs meaning will all influence comprehension. But meaning does not pass between writer and reader. It is represented by a writer in a text and constructed from a text by a reader. Characteristics of writer, text, and reader will all influence the resultant meaning." (Goodman, 1994)

The Writer

A. Writes to a specific audience.
B. Balances a sense of audience with his or her sense of how much background and detail must be provided.
C. Is constrained by his or her own values, concepts, and experiences taking into account the reader's needs, background, and interests.

The Reader

A. Engages in different kinds of reading:

1. Environmental (e.g., street signs)
2. Occupational (e.g., reading technical manuals)
3. Informational (e.g., TV Guide)
4. Recreational (e.g., novels)
5. Ritualistic (e.g., Bible)

B. Processing cycles:

1. Optical—scans and fixations
2. Perceptual—processing units (graphic features, letters, words, or phrases)
3. Syntactic—meaning predicting through knowledge of grammar
4. Semantic—concepts, experiences, and vocabulary

C. Cognitive strategies:

1. Initiation—decision to activate appropriate strategies and schemata
2. Sampling and selection—the reader samples and selects information which will be most productive and useful (select relevant data)
3. Inference—the reader guesses, on the basis of what is known, what information is needed but is not known
4. Prediction—the reader predicts what is coming syntactically and semantically

Source: Goodman, K.S. (1994). Reading, writing, and written texts: A transactional sociolinguistic view. In R.B. Ruddell, M.R. Ruddell, & Singer, H. (Eds.) *Theoretical models and processes of reading* (4th Edition). (pp. 1093-1130). Newark: International Reading Association.

5. Confirming and disconfirming—self-monitoring syntactic and semantic predictions
6. Correction—correcting false predictions
7. Termination—terminating reading because of text completion, disinterest, inability to comprehend, boredom, or lack of time.

D. Use of cueing systems (see next page)

(see next page)

Information Used During the Reading Process

I. Graphophonic Information

Graphic Information: Distinctive features of letters, letters, spelling patterns, words, sentences, paragraphs,...

Phonological Information: The speech sounds used by speakers of a language.

Phonic Information: The complex set of relationships between the graphic and phonological representations of the language. (Note: We are speaking of the relationships not an instructional program!)

II. Syntactic Information

Sentence Patterns: The grammatical sequences and interrelationships of language. *"The _____s _____ed the _____s."* is an example of a sentence pattern common in English.

Pattern Markers: The markers which outline the patterns.

> Function words: Those very frequent words which, though themselves relatively without definable meaning, signal the grammatical function of the other elements. (Examples: the, was, not, do, in, very, why . . .)
>
> Inflections: Those bound morphemes (affixes) which convey basically grammatical information (Examples: -ing, -ed, -s, pre-, . . .)
>
> Punctuation/Intonation: The system of marking and space distribution and the related intonational patterns. Pitch and stress variations and variable pauses in speech are represented to some extent by punctuation in writing.

Transformational Rules: These are not characteristic of the graphic input itself, but are supplied by the reader in response to what he perceives as its surface structure. They carry him to the deep structure and meaning. If he is to recognize and derive meaning from a graphic pattern, he must bring these grammatical rules into the process.

III. Semantic Information

Experience: The reader brings his prior experience into play in response to graphic input.

Concepts: The reader organizes the meaning he is reconstructing according to his existing concepts and reorganizes experience into concepts as he reads.

Vocabulary: A term for the ability of the child to sort out his experiences and concepts in relation to words and phrases in the context of what he is reading.

Source: Goodman, K.S. & Niles, O.S. (1970). Reading: Process and Program. National Council of Teachers of English: Urbana.

CHAPTER THREE

EMERGENT LITERACY

"Reading Readiness"/Emergent Literacy: Historical Perspectives

1. Prior to 1931, learning to read and beginning school in first grade were considered simultaneous events.

2. Holmes (1927) and Reed (1927) reported that many children failed first grade because they were not ready to read. Conclusion: Entering first graders were not ready to learn to read.

3. Reading "readiness" programs began to emerge throughout the U.S.

4. Morphett and Washburne (1931) "found" that the mental age of 6.5 was the appropriate age to begin reading instruction.

5. Programs throughout the country began assessing m.a. and postponed reading until the child had achieved the m.a. of 6.5.

6. Gates and Bond (1936), contrary to popular theory, identified the lowest achievers (N = 40) in four first grade classrooms and assigned them tutors. By June, all of the participating students were enjoying success in reading. The authors concluded: "This study emphasizes the importance of recognizing and adjusting to individual limitations and needs rather than merely changing the time of beginning. It appears that readiness for reading is something to develop rather than merely to wait for. . ."

7. Arnold Gesell (1940) supported the contentions of the postponement proponents. He believed that children were not ready to learn to read at the age of six and that instruction should be postponed until they were "ready". "Biological unfolding" explained Gesell's position—first graders were not at the "appropriate stage of development" for beginning to read.

8. Weird things began to happen in the name of "readying" children for reading: Visual discrimination of geometric forms, auditory discrimination of environmental sounds, teaching colors. . .

9. "Readiness" workbooks began accompying basal series providing non-reading activities.

10. Marie Clay (1966) coined the term emergent literacy. She maintained that children's knowledge of print, familiarity with books, listening skills, and understandings about writing and written material are all parts of basic literacy development that have been emerging in most children since infancy.

11. In 1966 we ignore Marie Clay.

12. Hillerich (1977) writes: "Traditionally, auditory discrimination activities have followed the same pattern of instruction in gross differences as visual discrimination activities, trying to teach children to recognize differences that have nothing to do with reading, trying to teach them to hear the difference between a roar of a jet and the rumble of a truck, between the slamming of a door and the ringing of a bell. Such activities are sheer nonsense for any three

year old who can speak his language, unless the point of such activities is merely to teach those children what is meant by 'same and different'."

13. Phil Dale's research on infants auditory discrimination abilities. . .

14. In the mid-1980's non-reading specific materials disappear.

15. Lapp and Flood (1992) write: "No longer is it believed that children can be readied for reading by running them through a kind of obstacle course, doing mental calisthenics with material that has no real connection to print. The expectation was that after spending time comparing circles to triangles and listening to various musical notes, children would then magically be ready to discriminate among various graphemes and phonemes and make meaning out of print. It was somewhat comparable to taking an entire physical education class and, after teaching them how to do sit-ups and jumping jacks, handing each student a pole and saying, "Now go vault 15 feet!" How well a child will do when handed the pole, or a page of print, depends on how much previous exposure he has had to those things and how comfortable he feels in attempting the task." (pp. 75-76)

Visual Discrimination of Geometric Forms

Visual Discrimination of...Who Knows?

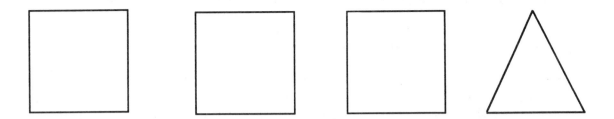

Visual Discrimination of Letter Forms

b   d   b   b

Visual Discrimination of Word Forms

man   man   ran   man

Early Literacy Events for Children

Oral Language Development

A. Encourage children to verbalize—answer their endless barrage of questions.

B. Talk with children at home—don't ignore their need to communicate.

C. Provide children with many out of home experiences—talk about what is seen.

D. Don't correct grammatical "errors" on the part of the child—there is a reason behind this.

Reading Experiences

A. Read to children at a very young age.

B. Mix reading material by introducing new stories while allowing the child opportunities to select old favorites.

C. Read a lot yourself—a young child will model your behavior and see that reading is a valued activity for a significant other.

D. Establish home libraries. Display your own books and create a library for the child.

E. Go to the library. Check out books. Let the child select some; you others.

F. Use Assisted Reading (or the Lap Method).

G. Make personal books with the child.

H. Develop Word Banks with the child.

I. Label the environment.

J. Provide many early writing experiences. The child should have ready access to paper, pencil, crayons, markers, etc.

K. Read predictable books to children. Bill Martin books are excellent!

Emergent Literacy

Emergent literacy is the concept that language, reading, and writing abilities evolve in a continuous fashion from birth and continue to grow throughout our lives. The term emergent literacy was coined by Marie Clay (1966) and has caught the attention of educators interested in early literacy.

"Emergent literacy assumes that the child acquires some knowledge about language, reading, and writing before coming to school. Literacy development begins early in life and is ongoing. There is a dynamic relationship between the communication skills; each influences the other in the course of development. Development occurs in everyday contexts of the home and community. Children at whatever age possess certain literacy skills, though these skills are not fully developed or conventional, as we recognize mature reading and writing to be. Emergent literacy acknowledges as rudimentary writing a child's scribble marks on a page, even is not a letter is discernible. The child who knows the difference between such scribbles and drawings certainly has some sense of the difference between writing and illustration. Similarly, when a child narrates a familiar storybook while looking at the pictures and print, and gives the impression of reading, we acknowledge that activity as legitimate literacy behavior, even though it cannot be called reading in the conventional sense." (Morrow, 1989)

Assumptions Regarding Emergent Literacy

1. Reading and writing are closely related processes and should not be artificially isolated for instruction.

2. Learning to read and write is essentially a social process and is influenced by a search for meaning.

3. Most preschool children already know a great deal about printed language without exposures to formal instruction.

4. Becoming literate is a continuous, developmental process.

5. Children need to act like readers and writers to become readers and writers.

6. Children need to read authentic and natural texts and write for personal reasons.

Literacy Development in Young Children

A. Pre-independent Reading Stages

Magical Stage

1. Displays an interest in handling books.

2. Sees the construction of meaning as magical or exterior to the print and imposed by others.

3. Listens to print read to him for extended periods of time.

4. Will play with letters or words.

5. Begins to notice print in environmental context (signs, labels).

6. Letters may appear in his drawings.

7. May mishandle books—observe them upside down. Damage them due to misunderstanding the purpose of books.

8. Likes to "name" the pictures in a book, e.g., "lion," "rabbit."

Self Concepting Stage

1. Self concepts himself as a "reader," i.e., engages in reading-like activities.

2. Tries to magically impose meaning on new print.

3. "Reads" or reconstructs content of familiar storybooks.

4. Recognizes his name and some other words in high environmental contexts (signs, labels).

5. His writing may display phonetic influence (invented spellings).

6. Can construct story meaning from pictorial clues.

7. Can not pick words out of print consistently.

8. Orally fills in many correct responses in oral cloze reading.

9. Rhymes words.

10. Increasing control over non-visual cueing systems.

11. Gives words orally that begin similarly.

From *Reading, Writing, and Caring* by Cochrane et al. Reprinted by permission of Orin Cochrane.

12. Displays increasing degree of book handling knowledge.

13. Is able to recall key words.

14. Begins to internalize story grammar (i.e., knows how stories go together).

Bridging Stage

1. Can write and read back his own writing.

2. Can pick out individual words and letters.

3. Can read familiar books of poems which could be totally repeated without the print.

4. Uses picture clues to supplement the print.

5. Words read in one context may not be read in another.

6. Increasing control over visual cueing system.

7. Enjoys chants and poems chorally read.

8. Can match or pick out words of poems or chants that have been internalized.

B. Independent Reading Stages

Take-Off Stage

1. Excitement about reading.

2. Wants to read to you often.

3. Realizes that print is the base for constructing meaning.

4. Can process (read) words in new (alternate) print situations.

5. Aware of and reads aloud much environmental print.

6. May exhibit temporary "tunnel vision" (concentrates on words and letters).

7. Oral reading may be word-centered rather than meaning-centered.

8. Increasing control over the reading process.

Independent Reading

1. Characterized by comprehension of the author's intended meaning.

2. Readers' construction of meaning relies on both print and own schemata.

3. Desire to read books to himself for pleasure.

4. Reads orally with meaning and expression.

5. May see print as a literal truth—what the print says is right.

6. Uses visual and non-visual cueing systems simultaneously.

7. Has internalized several different print grammars (e.g., fairy tales, general problem-centered stories, simple exposition).

Skilled Reader

1. Processes material further and further removed from his own experience.

2. Reading content and vocabulary become a part of his experience.

3. Can use a variety of print forms for pleasure.

4. Can discuss various aspects of a story.

5. Can read at varying and appropriate rates.

6. Can make inferences from print.

7. Challenges the validity of print content.

8. Wide variety of story grammar understanding.

Literacy Development and Pre-first Grade

A joint Statement of Concerns about Present Practices in Pre-first Grade Reading Instruction and Recommendations for Improvement

- Association for Childhood Education International

- Association for Supervision and Curriculum Development

- International Reading Association

- National Association for the Education of Young Children

- National Association of Elementary School Principals

- National Council of Teachers of English

Prepared by the Early Childhood and Literacy Development Committee of the International Reading Association.

Literacy Learning Begins in Infancy. Children Have Many Experiences with Oral and Written Language Before They Come to School.

- Children have had many experiences from which they build ideas about the functions and uses of oral and written language.

- Children have a command of language and of processes for learning and using language.

- Many children can differentiate between drawing and writing.

- Many children are reading environmental print, such as road signs, grocery labels, and fast food signs.

- Many children associate books with reading.

- Children's knowledge about language and communication is influenced by their social and cultural backgrounds.

- Many children expect that reading and writing will be sense-making activities.

Literacy Development and Early Childhood (Preschool through Grade 3). A joint statement prepared by the Early Childhood and Literacy Development Committee of the International Reading Association. Copyright © 1986 by the International Reading Association. All rights reserved.

Basic Premises of a Sound Pre-first Grade Reading Program

- Reading and writing at school should permit children to build upon their already existing knowledge of oral and written language.

- Learning should take place in a supportive environment where children can build a positive attitude toward themselves and toward language and literacy.

- For optimal learning, teachers should involve children actively in many meaningful, functional language experiences, including *speaking, listening, writing and reading*.

- Teachers of young children should be prepared in ways that acknowledge differences in language and cultural backgrounds, and should emphasize reading as an integral part of the language arts as well as of the total curriculum.

Concerns

- Many pre-first grade children are subjected to rigid, formal prereading programs with inappropriate expectations and experiences for their levels of development.

- Little attention is given to individual development or individual learning styles.

- The pressure of accelerated programs do not allow children to be risk takers as they experiment with written language.

- Too much attention is focused upon isolation skill development and abstract parts of the reading process, rather than on the integration of talking, writing and listening with reading.

- Too little attention is placed on reading for pleasure; therefore, children do not associate reading with enjoyment.

- Decisions related to reading programs are often based on political and economic considerations rather than on knowledge of how young children learn.

- The pressure to achieve high scores on tests inappropriate for the kindergarten child has led to undesirable changes in the content of programs. Activities that deny curiosity, critical thinking and creative expression are all too frequent, and can foster negative attitudes toward language communication.

- As a result of declining enrollment and reduction in staff, individuals with little or no knowledge of early childhood education are sometimes assigned to teach young children. Such teachers often select inappropriate methods.

- Teachers who are conducting pre-first grade programs without depending on commercial readers and workbooks sometimes fail to articulate for parents and other members of the public what they are doing and why.

Recommendations

1. Build instruction on what the child already knows about oral language, reading and writing. Focus on meaningful experiences and meaningful language rather than on isolated skill development.

2. Respect the language the child brings to school, and use it as a base for language and literacy activities.

3. Ensure feelings of success for all children, helping them to see themselves as people who enjoy exploring both oral and written language.

4. Provide reading experiences as an integrated part of the communication process, which includes speaking, listening and writing, as well as art, math and music.

5. Encourage children's first attempts at writing, without concern for the proper formation of letters or correct conventional spelling.

6. Encourage risk taking in first attempts at reading and writing, and accept what appear to be errors as part of children's natural growth and development.

7. Use reading materials that are familiar or predictable, such as well known stories, as they provide children with a sense of control and confidence in their ability to learn.

8. Present a model for children to emulate. In the classroom, teachers should use language appropriately, listen and respond to children's talk, and engage in their own reading and writing.

9. Take time regularly to read to children from a wide variety of poetry, fiction and non-fiction.

10. Provide time regularly for children's independent reading and writing.

11. Foster children's affective and cognitive development by providing them with opportunities to communicate what they know, think and feel.

12. Use developmentally and culturally appropriate procedures for evaluation, ones that are based on the objectives of the program and that consider each child's total development.

13. Make parents aware of the reasons for a broader language program at school and provide them with ideas for activities to carry out at home.

14. Alert parents to the limitations of formal assessments and standardized tests of pre-first graders' reading and writing skills.

15. Encourage children to be active participants in the learning process rather than passive recipients, by using activities that allow for experimentation with talking, listening, writing and reading.

CHAPTER FOUR

THE LANGUAGE EXPERIENCE APPROACH
A Tried and True Approach to Emergent Literacy

The Word Bank
in the Language Experience Approach

Materials Required

5 x 8 index cards

Index card file

Black marking pen

Personal word books

Procedures

1. Each day each child is asked to tell the teacher a new word he would like to learn to read.

2. That word along with other words housed in the child's Word Bank are practiced by the child. Words can be practiced in several ways:

   A. Oral recitation
   B. Several children combine the contents of their Word Banks and sort through the pile to find their own words (print names on backs of cards).
   C. The child may practice writing and saying their words while writing them on the chalkboard or in a tray containing cornmeal, fine sand, etc.
   D. The child may trace over the letters of the word while saying the parts of the word aloud. (For children having difficulty remembering words, use a black crayon for writing the words as this gives a surface by the child.)
   E. "D" above could be followed by the child trying to spell the word from memory on the chalkboard or another piece of paper.
   F. Two children may form a partner group. Each child tries to teach his own word to the other child.

3. Every other day the teacher reviews the words with each child. Words that are not remembered are not kept in the Word Bank but are dismissed as not being important enough to keep.

4. The teacher may want to put a check mark on the back of each word that is remembered. After the child has successfully read his word twenty times, the child may take that card home. (Parents should make a "big deal" about it.) The word can then be entered into his Personal Word Book to use in writing.

Extension

1. *Retrieving words from the floor*. The children's words (usually the words of a group or of half of the class is best) are placed on the floor face down. On the signal, each child is to find his own word, hold it up, and tell it to whoever is watching.

2. ***Claiming the cards.*** The teacher selects many words from the class, holds them up, and the child who "owns" each word claims it.

3. ***Telling stories spontaneously***. The child attempts to tell a story about his word. The story could be recorded and transcribed.

4. ***Classifying Words.*** Certain kinds of topics (e.g., desserts, television characters, funny words, places, activities) are chosen. Topics are selected according to classification. All of the children who have a "dessert" word, for example, would stand in one spot. The teacher might want to label the spot with a sheet of paper that says "dessert." Children who have words of other classifications also stand in their designated areas.

5. ***Relating words.*** Children play this game to see how some words are related to others. For example, someone may have the word "cake" and someone may have the word "knife." In such a case, a child may say that a knife can cut a cake.

6. ***Coauthorship.*** Two or more children can get together and combine their words to make longer and longer stories about their original words.

7. ***Pass-it-on stories.*** A group of no more than five children select words from their Word Banks. For example, they might select such Halloween words as "witch," "haunted," "bats," etc. The first child in a group will write the title; the next child, the starting of the story; each child in the group adds something new **to** the story. The teacher and children can chorally read the story upon completion.

8. ***Acting out words.*** If the word is conducive to "acting out," a child could dramatize his word for the others to guess.

The Use of the Language Experience Approach Group Experience Charts

1. Discuss some event or object of interest to the children. Inform the children that they will be writing a story about it.

2. The children cooperate in dictating the story to the teacher. The teacher writes down the story using the following methods:

    A. Use manuscript handwriting.
    B. Use a heavy writing instrument such as a felt tip pen.
    C. Use chart or butcher paper for recording.
    D. Use the language of the students—do not attempt to alter it.
    E. Make sure students see the words as they are being written.
    F. Try to adhere to the one important event/object and follow a sequence of events.
    G. In beginning each new sentence, emphasize the fact that you start on the left and proceed to the right.
    H. Emphasize the return sweep from the end of one line to the beginning of the next.

3. After the story has been completed, reread it as a choral exercise. Either you or a child may point to each word as it is read. It is important that the word being read is the same one being pointed to.

4. Have individual children take turns rereading the story sentence by sentence.

5. Experience stories are displayed in the room and reviewed on a daily basis for as long as deemed appropriate by the teacher.

Group Language: Experience Chart

We are going to have a Halloween party.

We will wear costumes.

Jimmy is going to be a ghost.

Robin is going to be a clown.

Frank is going to be a pirate.

Margaret is going to be a farmer.

Hanna is going to be a bunny.

Lena is going to be a rabbit.

Michael is going to be an owl.

Bart is going to be a cowboy.

Sharon is going to be a swan.

Anthony is going to be a monster.

We will have candy and cookies.

L.E.A. with an Individual Student

1. As with a group, find some event of interest to the students and ask the students to dictate a story to you.

2. As the student dictates, you write or type (primary typewriter for first and second graders; pica for third graders on up) the story on a piece of paper with the student positioned so that he or she may observe the writing or typing.

3. Have the student reread the story, with either you or the student (if able to do it properly) pointing to each word as it is read. Depending on the ability level of the student at this stage, the story may be reread sentence by sentence in varying order.

4. Let the student illustrate the story or apply stickers, pictures, or other decorations. Finally, the story should be placed in a booklet to be kept and reviewed frequently.

5. You may wish to duplicate the typewritten copies of these stories so that the student can cut them up and rearrange first the sentences and later the words within each sentence.

6. Bind groups of stories into booklets with illustrated covers and encourage children to exchange and read each other's booklets.

7. Gradually encourage the student to branch out into the reading of trade books.

LEA Activities

Whole Group

1. Make name labels with the first and last names of the students. Make a chart of the names as they appear on the labels. Have students match the labels with the names on the chart.

2. Make helper charts, using the names as they appear on the name labels. Have each student find his job, matching his/her name label with the chart. At first, pictures may be used to name the jobs. Later, pictures with words may be used, Finally, just words may be used.

3. Read stories to the children and leave the books where the children can look at them independently.

4. Use children's drawings and write sentences dictated by the children on them. Display the pictures or make books of them.

5. Bring something into the classroom that will generate language from the children. Develop a Group Experience Chart.

6. Take a walk to see fall colors, snow, or other seasonal conditions. On return, students list all the words they can that describe the subject of investigation. Students can write about their experience using their writing for reading and sharing.

7. Have a guest speaker speak to your class. The class prepares a list of questions for the speaker in advance. After the visit a thank you letter is composed.

Small Group

1. Have the children dictate a group story. Give each child a copy and have each read the story and underline the words he or she knows. At a later session, the process is repeated. The child again underlines the known words so that there are double lines under the ones remembered.

2. Use children's word banks to play word games such as: Match words that have the same beginning letters or beginning sounds; categorize words (e.g., animals, actions, feelings, etc.).

3. Show a film or filmstrip without narration. Have the children dictate the action while you copy this down.

4. Have the group members make puppets and write a script for a puppet play. The children will rehearse and eventually put on the play.

Individual Activities

1. Have the child dictate his own story while the teacher either carefully writes or types (using a primary typewriter) the child's story. The child practices the story and reads it to others.

2. Have each child make his/her own book of the stories he has dictated. When he/she gets to dictating stories several pages long, each story can be a book by itself.

3. After reading several alphabet books make up his/her own alphabet book.

4. Have each student grow a plant under special conditions such as no light, upside down, sideways, etc. A diary is kept of the project.

5. Have each student pretend he/she is from another planet. He/she may write a news account of his arrival on Earth.

Advantages of the Language Experience Approach

1. The first reading experiences are successful because they use the everyday language patterns of the children. Children who speak a nonstandard language are not penalized or made to feel inferior because they do not measure up verbally to the standard. Likewise, children whose language patterns are beyond those expected are not frustrated by the task of having to learn simpler sight words.

2. The approach is very economical.

3. Children can utilize the sight vocabulary they bring to school.

4. It is individualized in that each child is working at a level he/she can comprehend and with words he/she understands and can recognize.

5. Children learn that listening, writing, and spelling are a part of the reading process and, thus, that the language arts are interrelated.

6. Both phonics and sight words are used. Children see the relationship of sounds to the symbols used to represent them in writing.

7. Children learn to make choices and to function independently as they work with the skills.

8. Children feel their ideas are respected and accepted. This helps develop a positive self-image.

9. Motivation for and interest in reading are greatly increased, which may result in a positive attitude toward reading and creative expression.

10. Children are motivated to increase their spoken and written vocabulary.

11. When the approach is used with the basal program, the teacher may find that many of the words found in the preprimer may actually be learned before the books are presented.

12. Children may have insight into what goes into a story and can critique and discuss the writer's ideas because they, too, are writers.

13. Children's writings enable the teacher to learn more about the children themselves.

CHAPTER FIVE

TEACHING SIGHT WORDS

Teaching Sight Words to be Read in a Story

1. Write the word to be taught/learned on the chalkboard, overhead projector, chart paper, or sentence strip, using it in the context of a phrase or sentence. Underline the word.

2. After the students see the word, ask them to use word attack skills to pronounce it. It is better *not* to tell the students the word first, because then they do not have the opportunity to use independent word attack skills. If students cannot decode the word, pronounce it for them.

3. Discuss the meaning of the new word or how it is used in the sentence. Try to tie the new word to something in the children's experience. Draw from the children.

4. Write the word in isolation and ask the students to talk about what may help them remember it. Clues in the word's configuration, length, double letters, or initial sound can aid in memory. *Do not* have children look for little words within the new word being taught unless it is for the purpose of structural analysis. (EXAMPLE: *govern* in government is great; *go* in government is not helpful!)

5. Have the students write the word and say it as they write.

6. Have students compose new sentences using the word as it was used in the original context. Have the students read each other's sentences, emphasizing the word as it is pronounced.

Teaching a Sight Word: The McNinch Approach

1. *Demonstration*—the teacher selects a word of value for the student(s), which means that the word is in their oral-listening background. The word is presented in oral context in a normal language manner.

2. *Continued demonstration*—the orally presented word is presented in a written sentence or phrase context where all other words are in the students' sight vocabulary.

3. *Interaction*—the new word is written in isolation from the sentence, and the teacher directs the students to note features of the word such as beginning letter, ending letter, and number of letters and to see if it is the same as the identified word in the written sentence or phrase.

4. *Clarification*—students read the word in sentences or phrases where all other words are sight words. The focus is on students' oral reading of the context in which the word appears. If errors are made, they should be corrected immediately by the teacher and reread by the students.

5. *Application*—students read with teacher-direction meaningful context in which the word appears. The text should be familiar to the students and may include parts of a book, portions of a basal reader story, or excerpts from their language experience stories. The word under study should appear several times throughout the text to provide meaningful practice.

6. *Practice for mastery*—the teacher selects activities, such as games, flash cards, word banks, so forth, that can be kept short and briskly paced. Such practice activities should be structured to assure a high student success level so that correct responses are being practiced.

Miscellaneous Strategies for Teaching Sight Words

1. Use the sight words that cause difficulty in sentences. Underline the words that cause difficulty as in the following examples:

   A. I <u>thought</u> it was you.
   B. I could not go even <u>though</u> I have time.
   C. He ran right <u>through</u> the stop sign.

2. Pictures can be used to illustrate some words, such as *play, wash, work, small,* and *sing.* Use a picture with a sentence that describes it and the sight word underlined, or have the children make picture dictionaries of words.

3. Have the pupil write troublesome words on an index card and then pantomime the action described by the word.

4. Use words commonly confused in multiple-choice situations. Have the pupil underline the correct word:

   A. He wanted to (walk, wash) his clothes.
   B. He didn't know (when, what) to do.

5. Place one word that is different in a line of words. Ask the pupil to circle the one that says *what.*

   when   when   when   what   when   when   when

6. Develop and use games that reinforce identified sight words.

7. Use a *tachistoscope* to teach basic sight words.

Fernald Approach
(V.A.K.T. — Visual Auditory Kinesthetic Tactile)

Audience: Extremely disabled readers: Visually handicapped, neurologically impaired, children with visual-perceptual or visual processing problems.

Stage One

1. The teacher writes a student-chosen word with crayon on a large piece of paper (letters approximately two inches high).

2. The child traces the word with an index finger, saying each part of the word. This is repeated until the child can write the word without looking at the model.

3. After a few words are learned, the child dictates a short story to the teacher using many of his/her words. The story is typed for use on the next day. The words are kept in a folder.

4. Students are drilled each session on the words. When they recognize a word twenty consecutive times, the word is put in a permanent collection (e.g., personal dictionary) and reviewed two times a month.

Stage Two

1. Same as Stage One only tracing is omitted.

Stage Three

1. The child is involved in reading in books. When he or she does not recognize a word in print, it is written down.

2. The teacher records the word on an index card. The card is taught as a sight word.

Stage Four

1. The student is able to recognize new words from their resemblance to word/word parts he or she already knows on the basis of context.

Individual Vocabulary Method

The *Individual Vocabulary Method* is a modification of the Language Experience Approach (Word Banks) found to be particularly helpful with nonreaders of any age and individuals who have developed an aversion to books due to non-success.

1. The teacher begins by soliciting several important words from each child. (In later sessions, only one word is acquired.)

2. The words are written in neat manuscript handwriting on a large index card using a black marking pen.

3. At the beginning of each session, all of the students' cards are scattered on a table or the floor. The children find their own personal cards. (Hint: Write their names on the backs of the cards.)

4. The children then form reading partners and teach/learn each other's words. While this is going on, the teacher is working with individual children reviewing old words and generating/writing new ones.

5. A *Word Bank* is established. Children use their Word Banks to write stories. These stories are shared with the other students and housed in a class library to be read by others.

Shared Book Experiences

Skilled teachers can develop all of the concepts of print using Big Books. They model directionality by moving their hand across the pages; they demonstrate speech-print match and concept of word by pointing; and they begin to introduce the relationship of sound-symbol by careful voice pointing across words of different length (McCracken & McCracken, 1986; Slaughter, 1983). Typical shared book experiences include the following procedures:

1. After children have settled in a group around the teacher, he or she focuses children's attention on the cover, helps children to examine other aspects of the book (e.g., author, illustrator) and asks children to predict what might happen in the book.

2. The teacher reads the book aloud for pleasure.

3. Students and teacher discuss what happened in the story, focusing on response and comprehension.

4. In later encounters, the teacher rereads the book, pointing to the words and encouraging students to read along.

5. Students do repeated readings of the text, including taped read-alongs using small copies of the Big Book.

Predictable Books Technique

1. Teacher reads a predictable book aloud to the children. The teacher then rereads the book, encouraging students to join in when they can predict what will come next.

2. The story is transferred to a chart, without pictures to aid in the reading. Students reread the story from the chart. Then students match sentence strips from the story to sentences on the chart. Finally, students match individual words to the words in the story.

3. Students engage in choral rereading of the story from the chart. Word cards are presented randomly and the children match them to words in the story.

CHAPTER SIX

TEACHING CONTEXT CLUES

Context Clues

Context clues involve the use of two types of information systems: *Syntactic* and *semantic*. In using syntactic information to deduce an unknown word, we use our knowledge of the construction of the English language—grammar. Additionally, we may use the meaning of other words in the surrounding context to figure our unknown words—semantic information.

Some Kinds of Context Clues

1. *Direct explanation clues*. Often authors realize students will not know a word and place it in an explanation to help them. EXAMPLE: "*Lobbyists* got this name because they used to stand in a lobby or hall, outside the room where the laws were passed. They try to influence the laws that are made."

2. *Experience clues*. A student's own experience can help unlock an unknown word. EXAMPLE: "On any team, the members must *cooperate* by working together."

3. *Words in a series*. Often unknown words in a series can be decoded from clues. EXAMPLE: "There were marigolds, asters, and *chrysanthemums* among the flowers."

4. *Restatement*. To clarify, authors often repeat what they have stated. EXAMPLE: "In some places where fresh and salt water meet, as at the mouth of a river, the water is *brackish*. Brackish water is in between fresh and salt water in saltiness."

5. *Contrast and comparison*. Words such as *but* often give clues to word meaning. EXAMPLE: "Jerry smiled at Tim, but looked *disapprovingly* at me."

6. *Inference*. Surrounding words or sentences provide clues. EXAMPLE: "It was necessary to make sure that the coin was as old as the date said it was. Any *artifact* with writing on it is very important to historians."

Sample Context Clues Lessons

Place Clues Lesson

In this lesson we are trying to get children to notice syntactic cues intuitively without getting into a formal discussion of syntax. For example, suppose they are about to read a selection about an animal.

1. Write the sentence, *"The muddy nambol licked its paws and purred,"* on the chalkboard or overhead.

2. Have the children read the sentence.

3. Ask the children questions such as, "Do you think a nambol is an action word or a name of something? How can you tell? What would happen if we put nambol in a different position in the sentence? What do you think a nambol is?" Discuss why.

4. Extending the lesson: "Memory Clues"

    Ask them such questions as, "What does the word "muddy" make you remember? Do you think *that* memory will help you figure out what nambol means? What about the word "licked"? What does the word remind you of? Will it help you decide what nambol means? "Paws"? "Purred"?

Double Comma Clues Lesson

Children usually enjoy searching for these. They're straightforward and easy to spot—even for the reluctant reader.

1. Write the following sentences, for example, on the chalkboard or overhead: *"The gully, a deep ditch, was full of water."* and *"The galloon, or braid, was made of silver thread."*

2. Discuss with the children how the "comma-clued" words allude to the meaning of the unknown word.

Definition Clues Lesson

These are also easy and need very little demonstration by the teacher.

1. Write the following on the chalkboard or overhead projector:

    "The kind of poke I'm talking about is a small bag." and *"An ophthalmologist is a doctor who treats eye diseases."*

2. Discuss how they know the meanings of the underlined words.

Mood Clues Lesson

These are much more difficult to use and may require several demonstrations by the teacher.

1. Write the following sentences on the chalkboard or overhead projector:

   "The house was dark. The wind was howling through the cracks like ghosts. I was underline(terrified!)*"*

   and

   "First he'd lost his best friend. Then he's lost his bus fare. He was totally underline(depressed)*."*

2. Discuss how preceding context allude to the mood meanings of the underlined words.

Interpreter Clues Lesson

These are clues derived from the reader's interpretations or inferences and are the most difficult to demonstrate.

1. Write the following on the chalkboard or overhead:

   "His underline(opponent) *for the boxing match looked much stronger and bigger."*

   and

   "He was so angry his face was underline(florid)*."*

2. Discuss the possible meanings of the underlined words based upon the surrounding context and the children's own experiences.

Oral Cloze Lesson

This strategy is useful with younger or remedial students as an introduction to the use of context.

1. Read a story aloud to the children. As you read, omit certain words and replace them with a sound (nothing obscene). When the students hear the sound, they should write down the word they think should be inserted there. Younger children may respond orally.

2. Various responses should be shared and discussed in relation to them "making sense" or not.

Punctuation Clues Lesson

This lesson truly shows that punctuation **does** make a difference.

1. Write the following sentences on the chalkboard or overhead:

   The teacher said Harry was wrong.

   "The teacher," said Harry, "was wrong."

"Mary," said Betty, "likes chocolates."

Mary said Betty likes chocolates.

Henry Hamilton, Mary Louise John, and my cousin Tim went.

Henry, Hamiltom, Mary Louise, John, and my cousin Tim went.

Henry, Hamilton, Mary, Louise, John, and my cousin Tim went.

The Talk Through Method

This is a strategy that utilizes children's experiences and teacher questioning to discover the meaning of unknown vocabulary in context. It is a very informal technique, requires little teacher preparation, and is spontaneous. It also lends itself to normal classroom discussion and instruction.

1. The teacher presents new vocabulary to children in a sentence, preferably taken from the basal or literature story being read. Through questioning and discussion, the teacher "talks" children toward the discovery of the meanings of words. In this way teachers lead children to develop a habit of trying to discover the meanings of words through their own experiences and knowledge gained from the sentence.

2. When particular words appear that children may have difficulty in recognizing and knowing, you may want to read the sentence to the children and use this technique. A sample example and dialogue are provided below.

    Example: *"Cats are endlessly, voraciously curious and seem to find their way to hidden treasures around the house, when even their owners cannot remember where to find them!"*

    Dialogue:

    Teacher: "What does the sentence tell you about the word voraciously?"

    Children: "It is something cats have to do."

    Teacher: "What do cats who are voraciously curious do?"

    Children: "Look everywhere and find things people can't."

    Teacher: "Are other animals voraciously curious? Are you?"

    Children: "Our dog did the same thing with my shoe!"

    Teacher: "What do you think voraciously might mean?"

3. The teacher could continue the discussion by having children list other examples of voracious behavior from their experiences.

Activities That Facilitate the Use of Context Clues

1. Read a sentence aloud and omit an "unknown" word, but tell the students the beginning sound. Ask students what they think the word is and why they came to that conclusion. Discuss the *whys* of the choices. Other students will be aided by the "how to do it" of their peers.

2. Provide examples showing that context clues may *precede* or *follow* the unknown word.

    Preceding: "People who write about famous persons, places, and events of the past are called *historians*."

    Following: "Among them are *antibodies*. These fight germs."

3. Provide examples showing that context clues may be a *phrase, sentence,* or *paragraph*.

    Phrase: "The day was *sweltering*, too hot for any fun."

    Sentence: "She *announced* loudly to everyone that she was leaving."

    Paragraph: "He held the *questionnaire* in his hand. 'I need your help', he stated. 'I don't know how to fill out the answers to all of these questions. Why are they asking so many?"

4. Have students search through some of their favorite books to see how skillfully authors may provide many context clues.

5. Have students write sentences to exchange with their classmates where the context explains the word, and where choices are provided.

    EXAMPLE: "Dr. Sippola has a way of making the most difficult reading concepts understandable. His *lucid* explanations help us to understand them."

    interesting   clear   dumb

6. Demonstrate that it is possible to derive the meaning of words from their context. Show specific examples:

    "The careless boy did his work in a *haphazard* manner."

    "He felt that although his work was *imperfect*, it was still good."

    "They called in a *mediator* to help settle the problems between labor and management."

7. Begin by constructing sentences or short paragraphs in which words that the student should be able to determine by context are omitted. In place of each key word, insert an initial consonant and then *x*'s for the rest of the letters in the words.

    "When Jan is in a hxxxx, he always rxxx home from school."

    "He read the bxxx and found that reading was fxx."

---

8. Make tape recordings in which key words are omitted. Give the pupil a copy of the script and have him fill in the blank spaces as the tape is played.

9. Have the student practice reading up to a word, sounding at least the first sound, and then reading several words following the unknown word.

   "A cow and her c_____ drank from the water hole."

   "The p_____ arrested the robber."

10. Make a series of sentences using words that are spelled alike but may have different pronunciations or meanings.

    "She *read* the book."
    "She will *read* the story."

    "It was made out of *lead*."
    "She had the *lead* in the play."

Using the CLOZE Procedure with Passages

One of the most effective strategies to use in facilitating the use of context clues is by using the CLOZE procedure. Valmont (1983) suggests the following guidelines for the use of the CLOZE procedure with passages:

1. Generally, do not delete words from either the first or last sentence of the passage.

2. Be clear about your reasons for deleting a word. Although when the CLOZE procedure is used for testing, words are deleted at regular intervals (e.g., a blank replaces every fifth word), this same technique *should not be used for instructional purposes*.

3. Especially while introducing the use of context, delete words most students will be able to guess correctly through applying knowledge of passage meaning.

4. In the early stages also try to delete words used over and over again in the passage. Delete them for the first time only after they have already appeared several times.

5. In general, only delete words in the students' oral vocabulary, those representing concepts familiar to them.

6. In the early stages, delete categories of words, such as nouns, verbs, adjectives, and adverbs, for which the children will be able to generate many different possibilities. In later stages, when more precision is being sought, delete other categories of words such as prepositions, where fewer alternatives can be suggested.

7. If you want to give students more within-sentence context, or make the task easier, delete words at the end of the sentence.

8. If you want students to practice using context clues coming after the deleted word, remove words from the beginning of the sentence.

A Moose Named Bill

Once upon a time there was a moose named Bill. Bill was a rather _____ moose. One day Bill decided that _____ would cause some trouble in downtown Anchorage. First Bill ate all of the birch_____ in a park. After he ate all of the birch trees in the park, he _____ into a souvenir shop. In the shop he_____ up all of the tee-shirts. After he was _____ with the souvenir shop, he_____ all of the parking meters over on Fourth Avenue. This made a _____ of shoppers happy.

The shop owners and police _____ that they had had enough of Bill the Moose. They came up with a plan. They hired Mary Moose, a recent centerfold in *Playmoose Magazine,* to lure Bill_____ a trap. She began to make _____ noises down by the statue of Captain Cook. Bill charged in her direction. When he _____ close to Mary, she jumped _____ of the way. Bill couldn't _____ and wound up on an ice flow. Bill floated out to Fire Island and has never made it back to Anchorage since.

Sample MAZE Procedure

1. The _____ ran down the road.

   dog   at   boat

2. A _____ boy was waiting at the door.

   man   think   tall

3. I wish I _____ jump like that.

   limb   clod   could

4. The lone student in WSU's library was informed that both

   of the university's _____ had been checked out.

   girls   books   sheep

CHAPTER SEVEN

TEACHING STRUCTURAL ANALYSIS

Structural Analysis

In studying structural analysis as a method of identifying words, we will be working with *morphemes*. Morphemes are the smallest units of our language that have meaning. The word *dog* is one morpheme. The word *football* is composed of two morphemes: *foot* and *ball* (two meaning units). The word *unkindly* deals with three meaning units: un + kind + ly. The word *books* has two morphemes: book + s. The *s* changes the meaning of the word.

Kinds of Structural Clues Used by Readers

1. Recognizing words within *compound words*. Examples: *rainfall, snowmobile, basketball, freeway*.

2. Recognizing *suffixes*. Examples: *runs, running* (affects grammatical function); *payer, payee* (affects meaning).

3. Recognizing *contractions* (Lamaze???). Examples: *can't, wouldn't, won't, I'd*.

4. Recognizing *root words* (the smallest unit in which the meaning shared by related words exists). Examples: *teach* is the root for *teacher, teaching,* and *teaches*.

5. Recognizing *word families* (a group of words whose roots are either identical (*teach, teacher, teaching*) or of the same origin (*inspect, spectacles, spectator*).

6. Recognizing prefixes (a unit of one or more letters that is placed before a root word to affect its meaning). Examples: un*happy*, a*moral*.

7. Recognizing words that have both *prefixes* and *suffixes*. Examples: pre*arrange*ment, bi*color*ed.

Use of Structural Analysis: Greek and Latin Influences

PREFIX	MEANINGS	EXAMPLES
anthropo-	man	anthropology
aqua-	water	aquarium
auto-	self, self-propelled	automatic, automobile
bi-	two	bilingual
biblio-	book, of books	bibliography
bio-	life, of living things	biology
cosmo-	world, universe	cosmopolitan
geo-	earth	geology
heter(o)	different, other	heterogeneous
homo-	man	homicide
homos	same, equal	homogeneous
hydro-	water, hydrogen	hydroelectric
mal-	bad, badly, wrong	malice, maltreatment
micro-	small	microfilm
mono-	one, alone	monosyllable
neuro-	nervous system, of a nerve	neurotic
omni-	all, everywhere	omnipresent
per-	through	permeate, perforate
phil(o)	love	philanthropy
photo-	light, produced by light	photograph
poly-	many	polysyllable
tele-	far off	telephone

ROOT	MEANINGS	EXAMPLES
audire	to hear	audience
cedere	to move, go	precede
cyclo	circle	cycle
dicere	to speak, tell	predict
gram	something written	telegram
graph	something that records or describes	phonograph

ROOT	MEANINGS	EXAMPLES
logos	speech, reason, study of	monologue, logic, geology
mare	sea	marine
meter	measure	thermometer
mittere	to send	transmit
mobilis	movable	mobile
phobia	fear or hatred of	claustrophobia
phonos	sound	phonics
porta	door	porthole
portare	to carry	import
scire	to know	science
scope	instrument for observing	telescope
scribere	to write	postscript
sonus	sound	supersonic
spectare	to see, look at	spectacles
tenere	to hold, have	tenacious
visio	sight	vision

1. If a person were described as a *bibliophile*, what would that tell you about him?

2. If a picture had to be taken with a *telephoto* lens, what would that indicate?

3. What is the difference between someone who is *omniscient* and someone who is *prescient*?

4. In a chemistry laboratory, it is likely that you would find *aqueous* solutions. What are they?

5. What do you suppose a *micrometer* is?

6. What might a *cyclometer* be?

7. If a person is described as having *aquaphobia*, what does that reveal?

8. What is *sonorous* metal?

9. Were an *omnibus* bill passed by a legislature, what kind of bill would it be?

10. Is something that is *malodorous* appealing? Why (not)?

11. What would an *omniverous* reader be?

12. Who would be interested in having an *aqualung*?

Sample Exercises Involving Structural Analysis

1. Put the parts in the right order to make a big word.

    agree dis ment_____

    ed develop un _____

    less ly care _____

2. The words in each of the groups below begin with the same letters. Sometimes these letters for the prefixes un-, in-, dis-, which often mean "opposite of" or "not." Check each word below that contains a prefix meaning "opposite of" or "not."

_____ unable	_____ incorrect	_____ dislike
_____ unjust	_____ interrupt	_____ discourteous
_____ union	_____ inexpensive	_____ discontent
_____ uncle	_____ inconvenient	_____ disciple
_____ unbroken	_____ insect	_____ distrust

3. Use the appropriate prefix or suffix to make a word that could be substituted for the underlined word in each sentence.

    Andy jerked on the rope, but he was <u>not able</u> to tighten the knot.

    _____able

    When it rained, the wheels of the wagon were <u>covered with mud</u>.

    mud_____

    The first shingle that Andy made was <u>not perfect</u>, but the next one was excellent.

    _____perfect

4. Either of the two words beneath each sentence could complete the sentence, but only one of them answers the question asked. Read the incomplete sentence and the two words. Then read the question and draw a line under the word that answers it.

    The label on the jar stated that the fruit was _____.

    presweetened   unsweetened

    Which word would indicate that nothing has been added to sweeten the fruit?

The patient was _____ when he was taken to the hospital.

unconscious   semiconscious

Which word would indicate that the patient was partly aware of things?

Mike is very _____ about returning library books when they are due.

careful   careless

Which word would indicate that Mike probably pays many library fines?

CHAPTER EIGHT

TEACHING PHONIC ANALYSIS

Most Commonly Taught Phonic Elements

Consonant Sounds

b c d f g h j k l m n p qu r s t v w y z

Consonant Blends

bl br cl cr dr dw fl fr gl gr pl pr sc sk sm sn sp st sw tr tw scr str

Double Consonants

gg - egg
ss - miss
tt - putt
ll - tell
dd - odd
ff - gruff
nn - dinner
tt - attend
pp - suppose

Silent Consonants

h - heir, hour
gh - ghost
kh - khaki
rh - rhythm
gn - gnaw
kn - knee
wr - wrong
pn - pneumonia
ps - psychology
pt - ptomaine
g - weigh, high
b - dumb
l - talk
t - listen

Single Vowels (long sound)

a - late
e - fete
i - bite
o - note
u - mute, lute

Schwa (de-emphasized short u)

local, secret, imitate, polite

Vowel Digraphs

au - auto
aw - raw
oo - moon
oo - book
ee - week
ei - ceiling
ie - pie
ea - each
ai - aim
oa - boat
ey - key
ay - say
ue - glue

Consonant Digraphs

th - thank, this
sh - shirt
ch - chip
ph - phone
gh - enough
ng - dang

Single Vowels *(short sound)*

a - bat
e - met
i - bit
o - got
u - but

Diphthongs

ou - out
ow - owl
ow - slow
oi - soil
oy - boy
ew - few
ew - new

Teach phonetic generalizations that apply approximately 75% of the time.

The Utility of Phonic Generalizations in Grades One Through Six

From Clymer's Study

Generalizations	No. of Words Conforming	No. of Exceptions	% of Utility Clymer	Bailey	Emans
1. When there are two vowels side by side, the long sound of the first is heard, the second is usually silent.	309 (bead)	377 (chief)	45	34	18
2. When a vowel is in the middle of a one-syllable word, the vowel is short.	403	249	62	71	73
Middle Letter	191 (dress)	84 (scold)	69	78	81
One of the middle 2 letters in a word of 4 letters	191 (rest)	115 (told)	59	68	71
One vowel within a word of more than four letters	26 (splash)	30 (fight)	46	62	42
3. If the only vowel letter is at the end of a word, the letter usually stands for a long sound.	23 (he)	8 (to)	75	76	33
4. When there are two vowels, one is long and the e is silent.	180 (bone)	134 (done)	63	57	63
5. The r gives the preceding vowel a sound that is neither long nor short.	484 (barn)	134 (wire)	78	86	82
6. The first vowel is usually long and the second silent in the digraphs ai, ea, oa, and ui.	179	92	66	60	58
ai	43 (nail)	24 (maid)	64	71	83
ea	101 (bead)	51 (head)	66	55	82
oa	34 (boat)	1 (cupboard)	97	95	85
ui	1 (suit)	16 (build)	6	10	0
7. In the phonogram ie, the i is silent, and the e has a long sound.	8 (field)	39 (friend)	17	31	23
8. Words having double e usually have the long sound.	85 (seem)	2 (been)	98	87	100
9. When words end with silent e, the preceding a or i is long.	164 (cake)	103 (have)	60	50	48

From Spache and Spache, *Reading in the Elementary School*, 5th Ed. Copyright 1986 by Allyn and Bacon. Reprinted by permission.

10. In ay, the y is silent and gives a its long sound.	36 (play)	10 (always)	78	88	100
11. When the letter i is followed by the letters gh, the i usually stands for its long sound, and the gh is silent.	22 (high)	9 (neighbor)	71	71	100
12. When a follows w in a word, it usually has the sound a as in was.	15 (watch)	32 (swam)	32	22	28
13. When e is followed by w, the vowel sound is the same as represented by oo.	9 (blew)	17 (sew)	35	40	14
14. The two letters ow make the long o sound.	50 (own)	35 (down)	59	55	50
15. W is sometimes a vowel and follows the vowel digraph rule.	50 (crow)	75 (threw)	40	33	31
16. When y is the final letter in a word, it usually has a vowel sound.	169 (currency)	32 (repay)	84	89	98
17. When y is used as a vowel, it sometimes has the sound of long i.	29 (cry)	170 (surgery)	15	11	4
18. The letter a has the same sound (o) when followed by l, w, u.	61 (awning)	65 (awake)	48	34	24
19. When a is followed by r and final e, we expect to hear the sound heard in care.	9 (flare)	1 (are)	90	96	100
20. When c and h are next to each other, they make only one sound.	103 (church)	0	100	100	100
21. Ch is usually pronounced as it is in kitchen, catch and chair not like sh.	99 (pitch)	5 (chef)	95	87	67
22. When c is followed by e or i, the sound of s is likely to be heard.	66 (ice)	3 (ancient)	96	92	90
23. When the letter c is followed by o or a, the sound of k is likely to be heard.	143 (canal)	0	100	100	100
24. The letter g often has a sound similar to that of j in jump when it precedes the letter i or e.	49 (genius)	28 (eager)	64	78	80
25. When ght is seen in a word, gh is silent.	30 (tight)	0	100	100	100

26. When a word begins kn, the k is silent.	10 (knit)	0		100	100	100
27. When a word begins with wr, the w is silent.	8 (wrap)	0		100	100	100
28. When two of the same consonants are side by side, only one is heard.	334 (dollar)	3 (accept)		99	98	91
29. When a word ends in ck, it has the same last sound as in look.	46 (neck)	0		100	100	100

Useful Phonics Generalizations

1. Single Consonants: Reading Grade Level 1.

   Generally, consonants are dependable in sound. They include *b, d, f, h, j, k, l, m, n, p, r, s, t, v, w, x,* and *z. C* and *g* have two common sounds.

2. **Consonant Digraphs:** Reading Grade Level 1.

   These refer to two consonants that, when together, make one sound. Common digraphs are *sh, ch, ck, ph,* and *th* (as in *thy* and *thigh*). *Qu* is sometimes considered a digraph.

3. Consonant Blends: Reading Grade Level 2.

   These are two or three consonants blended together for pronunciation. Beginning blends include *st, gr, cl, sp, pl, tr, br, dr, bl, fr, fl, pr, cr, sl, sw, gl, str.* Ending blends include *nd, nk, nt, lk, ld, rt, nk, rm, rd, rn, mp, ft, lt, ct, pt, lm.*

4. **Single Vowels, Long and Short Vowels:** Reading Grade Levels 2-3.

   Long vowels are sometimes called "free" or "glided" forms. Short vowels are called "checked" or "unglided." Long vowels occur (a) when a vowel is followed by a consonant and an *e,* the *e* is usually silent (e.g., *rate*), and (b) when a vowel ends a word or syllable (e.g., *be, begin*). Short vowels occur when a single vowel is followed by one or more consonants (e.g., *rat*). Words like *rate* are often contrasted to pairs such as *rat.*

5. "R"-*Controlled Vowels*: Reading Grade Levels 2-3.

   These include *ar, er, ir, or,* and *ur.* Note that *er, ir,* and *ur* sound alike.

6. *Vowel Combinations:* Reading Grade Levels 2-3.

   Dependable combinations include *oo, ai, ee, oi, aw, ay, ew,* and *ou.* Less dependable combinations are *ea* (seat, bear), *ow,* (cow, low), *oo* (boot, look).

7. **Hard and Soft "C" and "G":** Reading Grade Level 3.

   Soft "c" as in *city.* Hard "c" as in *cat.* Soft "g" as in *general.* Hard "g" as in *gold.* Generally, soft sounds are followed by *e, i,* and *y.* Hard sounds occur elsewhere. These principles are more dependable for *c* than for *g.*

8. **Silent Letters:** Reading Grade Levels 3-4.

   When consonant combinations cannot be pronounced together, the second is *usually* pronounced (as in *know* and *would*). However, when the second consonant is *h,* the first consonant is pronounced (as in *ghost*).

Source: Richek, M.A., List, L.K., and Lerner, J.W. (1989). Reading problems: Assessment and teaching strategies. 2nd ed. Prentice Hall: Englewood Cliffs.

"Exemplary" Phonics Instruction

1. Builds on a child's rich concepts about how print functions.

    1. Children need to know that phonics can assist them in decoding only as a part of the bigger picture of reading.
    2. Some children need very little phonic instruction. Many children who have had a rich literary background have figured out as much phonics as they need on their own.
    3. Good readers know what "reading" is.

2. Builds on a foundation of phonemic awareness.

    1. Children need to be aware of the sounds in spoken words.
    2. (Phonemic segmentation activities should help.)

3. Is clear and direct.

    1. Provide direct instruction with real words.
    2. Phonic workbooks are a no-no.

4. It is integrated into a total reading program.

    1. Real reading is the most important facet of any reading program. Phonics is but a small portion of the reading program.
    2. Phonics instruction should be tied to real stories. isolated phonics instruction without relevant application is, also, a no-no.

5. Focuses on reading words, not learning rules.

    1. Children, when using phonics, apply their skills by analogy. For example, van is like man ... so is ban, can, fan, pan, ran, and tan.
    2. Only teach high utility, high frequency patterns.

6. May include onsets and rimes.

    1. An onset is the part of the syllable before the vowel.
    2. A rime is that part from the vowel onward.

    Nearly 500 words can be derived from the following 37 rimes:

-ack	-ain	-ake	-ale	-all	-ame
-an	-ank	-ap	-ash	-at	-ate
-aw	-ay	-eat	-ell	-est	-ice
-ick	-ide	-ight	-ill	-in	-ine
-ing	-ink	-ip	-ir	-ock	-oke
-op	-or	-ore	-uck	-ug	-ump
-unk					

Adapted from Stahl, S. (1992). Saying the "p" word: Nine guidelines for exemplary phonics instruction. *The Reading Teacher.* 45(8), 618–625.

7. May include invented spelling practice.

    1. Only one study (Clarke, 1989,) has been done on the efficacy of invented spelling on decoding and comprehension. Results were favorable.

8. Develops independent word recognition strategies, focusing attention on the internal structure of words.

    1. "The object of phonics instruction is to get children to notice orthographic patterns in words and to use those patterns to recognize words."
    2. Writing helps children analyze words for patterns.

9. Develops automatic word recognition skills so that students can devote their attention to comprehension, not words.

    1. Children need to be able to use their attention upon meaning rather than on struggling with word recognition.
    2. Good phonics instruction is also over relatively quickly. Anderson, Hiebert, Wilkinson, and Scott (1985) recommends that phonics instruction be completed by the end of the second grade. This may even be too long. Stretching phonics instruction out too long, or spending time on teaching the arcane aspects of phonics—the schwa, the silent k, assigning accent to polysyllabic words—is best a waste of time.

Phonemic Segmentation

Definition: Phonemic segmentation is defined as the ability to isolate, in proper sequence, the individual sounds found in a word.

Lewkowicz (1980) found that this ability, plus blending were closely related to reading success and should be taught to early readers. However, a number of research studies (Adams, 1990; Allan, 1982; Anderson, et al, 1985; Ehri & Wilce, 1985; Liberman et al., 1977; Wallach, Wallach, Dozier, & Kaplan, 1977) have demonstrated that phonemic segmentation ability is often difficult for young children to acquire.

Instructional Possibilities

Burns, Roe, and Ross (1988) describe a technique involving the auditory modality. It involves the following:

1. The teacher says a familiar word slowly and deliberately.

2. The children are asked to repeat the word in the same way and tap on the table or put down a marker for each sound that is heard.

3. Later, the teacher should help the child associate letters with the sounds by constructing a response sheet where children write in the corresponding graphemes to the phonemes they hear the teacher pronounce.

Calkins (1986) described a technique she calls **word rubber-banding** which involves children in attempts at trying to stretch out words so as to be able to isolate the individual sounds to aid in invented spelling. For example, the word run would be stretched into rrrrruuuuuuuuunnnnnnnn to allow the writer to identify and segment the word into the phonemic sounds.

A Sample Phonics Lesson
Featuring Holistic and Direct Instruction

Objective: Building sound-symbol relationships: Initial consonant sound: /b/

Purpose

1. Explain to the students that they will be learning about the sound the letter "b" may stand for. Add that this knowledge will help them in reading words in stories.

Whole

1. Read the book *The Berenstain B Book* to the children.

Direct

1. Write the words *bat, bad,* and *bag* on the chalkboard. Underline the letter *b* in each of the words.

2. SAY: "I've written three words on the board that begin with the same letter. Each word begins with the same sound, too. I will read each of the words to you. See if you can hear how they sound alike at the beginning."

3. As you read each word, point to the letter *b*.

4. SAY: "I see the letter *b* at the beginning of each of the words. What sound did you hear at the beginning of each of the words?

5. Have the children respond. Direct the responses according to correctness.

6. Separate the words into onsets and rimes:

    b at
    b ad
    b ag

7. Say each onset and rime separately. Then blend them together. (modeling)

8. Have the children do the same as you point.

9. Have the children use their word banks to select all of their words that begin with the letter b.

10. As each child reads you those words, list them on a b chart made from butcher paper.

11. Once step 10 is completed, have the children read the words from the chart (you may want the word author to take the lead!).

12. Re-emphasize the sound symbol relationship between b & /b/.

Whole

1. Do rehearsal reading (teacher and children reading together) of the book *The Berenstain Bears and Too Much Birthday.*

2. Children do Partner Reading re-reading *The Berenstain Bears and Too Much Birthday.*

Trachtenburg's (1990) Analytic Phonics Method

1. The teacher reads a literature selection that contains many examples of the phonic element in question to the group. Students may discuss or dramatize the story when the teacher has finished.

2. The teacher introduces the phonic element that is the target for the lesson by explaining that the children are going to learn one sound for' a specific letter or letter combination.

3. The teacher writes a portion of the story that contains the target element on the chalkboard, overhead transparency, or chart paper. The teacher reads this portion of the story aloud, pausing to underline the words containing the target element.

4. The teacher identifies the sound involved and asks the children to read the story portion with him or her, listening for the sound. The teacher may suggest a key word that will help them remember the sound in the future.

5. The teacher guides practice with the new sound, making use of a mechanical device (see below) in which initial consonants can be varied while the medial vowel and ending consonant remain the same.

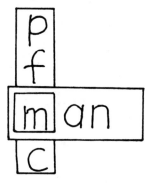

6. The teacher presents another book that has numerous examples of the phonic element. Children are then allowed to read this book independently, read it in unison from a big book, or read it with a partner.

Adapted from Trachtenburg, P. (1990). Using children's literature to enhance phonic instruction. *The Reading Teacher* 43(9), 648–654.

A General Model to Symbol-Sound Instruction

1. **What**

   A. Explain what the children will be learning.

2. **Why**

   A. Explain why this is important.

3. **How**

   A. Write two or three examples of words containing the phonic element. These should be words children have in their word banks or in initial reading materials.
   B. Ask the students what the words have in common.
   C. Either you or the children read the words aloud.
   D. Ask the students if the letter(s) have the same sound in all of the words.
   E. Identify the letter sound and explain that this is the usual sound for this letter or cluster of letters.
   F. Have the children use the letter or cluster of letters to invent the spelling of two or three new words.

4. **Provide guided practice**

   A. Write several more examples on the board.
   B. Ask the children to read the new words to you.
   C. Should blending cause a problem, have the children participate in "say it slow" and "say it fast" exercises.
   D. Provide children with sentences where a word containing the targeted phonic element is deleted (e.g., "The boy _____ on the chair."; "The dog chased the _____.")

5. **When**

   A.
   Remind the students to use this skill in combination with context to decode unknown words.

6. **Provide for independent practice**

   A. Students should try to apply their new knowledge as they read everyday texts (or the Trachtenburg recommended books).

Adapted from Taylor, B., Harris, L.A., Pearson, P.D., Garcia, G. (1995). Reading difficulties: Instruction and assessment. McGraw-Hill: New York.

First-Grade Phonics Checklist

Phonemic Awareness

_____ segmenting   _____ blending   _____ rhyming

Consonants

_____ b   _____ f   _____ j   _____ m   _____ qu   _____ t

_____ c(k)   _____ g   _____ k   _____ n   _____ r   _____ v

_____ d   _____ h   _____ l   _____ p   _____ s   _____ w

Blends	**Digraphs**	**Rimes**
_____ bl	_____ ch	_____ at
_____ dr	_____ sh	_____ ill
_____ fl	_____ th	_____ op
_____ st	_____ wh	_____ ate
_____ tr		_____ ike
		_____ ay

Short Vowels	**Long Vowels**	**Rules**
_____ a (fan)	_____ a (came, pail)	_____ CVC
_____ e (web)	_____ e (be, feet, eat)	_____ CVCe
_____ i (sit)	_____ i (ice, bite)	_____ r-controlled
_____ o (not)	_____ o (go, soap)	
_____ u (cup)	_____ u (mule)	

Source: Tompkins, G.E. (1997). Literacy for the 21st century. Merrill: Columbus.

Another Sample of a Phonic Lesson: bl

1. Developing awareness of hearing the sound:

    A. Say, "Listen to these words. Each of them begins with the **bl** sound. Circle **bl** on each word on your paper as you hear the sound. Blow, blue, blunder," etc.

2. Developing awareness of seeing the sound:

    A. Tell the student to circle all of the words in passage that begins with **bl**.

3. Providing practice in saying words with the **bl** sound:

    A. Pronounce each word and have students pronounce it after you.

    blow   blue   blunder   bleed   blast

4. Providing practice in blending the **bl** sound with common phonograms:

    A. Teach or use several phonograms with which students are already familiar such as **ock** and **ush.** Put the **bl** in one column, the phonogram in a second column, and the two combined in a third column as follows:

    | bl | ock | block |
    | bl | ack | black |
    | bl | ur | blur |
    | bl | under | blunder |

    Instruct the student to say **bl** (the two letters and not the sound) and then the phonogram (this time sound represented by the letters in the phonogram) and then the word formed by the two.

5. Asking the student to make a list of some words that begin with **bl**. If this is too difficult, provide a list of some phonograms from which some **bl** words can be formed. Ask the student to say each word as he or she writes it.

6. Providing practice in reading **bl** words. Have the child read a short story containing lots of **bl** words.

A Drim Kum Tru

If he had not tried to rush it, George Bernard Shaw might have succeeded in giving the English-speaking peoples a phonetic alphabet. Says the *Smithsonian Torch*, a slim house organ put out by the Smithsonian Institution for the museum set: "We are in complete accord with Bernard Shaw's campaign for a simplified alphabet. But instead of immediate drastic legislation, we advocate a modified plan.

"In 1957, for example, we would urge the substituting of 'S' for soft 'C'. Sertainly students in all sites of the land would be reseptive to this.

"In 1958, the hard 'C' would be replased by 'K' sinse both letters are pronounsed identikally. Not only would this klarify the konfusion in the minds of spellers, but typewriters and linotypes kould all be built with one less letter and all the manpower and materials previously devoted to making the 'C's' kould be used to raise the national standard of living.

"In the subsequent blaze of publisity it would be announsed that the troublesome 'PH' would be henseforth written 'F'. This would make words like "fonograf" 20 persent shorter in print.

"By 1959, the publik interest in a fonetik alfabet kan be expekted to have reatshed a point where more radikal prosedures are indikated. We would urge at that time the elimination of al double leters whitsh have always ben a nuisanse and desided deterent to akurate speling.

"We would al agre that the horible mes of silent 'E's' in our language is disgrasful. Therefore, in 1961, we kould drop thes and kontinu to read a writ merily along as though we wer in an atomik ag of edukation. Sins by this tim it would be four years sins anywun had used the leter 'C', we would then sugest substituting 'C' for 'Th'.

"Kontinuing cis proses year after year, we would eventuali hav a reali sensibl writen language By 1975, wi ventyur tu sa cer wud bi no mor uv ces teribli trublsum difikultis. Even Mr. Shaw, we beliv, sud bi hapi in ce noleg cat his drims finali kam tru."

Using Children's Literature to Enhance Phonics Instruction

Teachers are currently attuned to the instructional potential of using children's literature to teach beginning reading. Proponents advocate the use of whole stories, value a meaning emphasis, and believe that through repeated readalongs, assisted reading (Hoskisson, 1975), and shared-book experiences (Holdaway, 1982), many children will begin to read spontaneously. However, there is also strong support for early, intensive instruction in phonic analysis to help students achieve independence in word recognition (Calfee & Drum, 1986).

Fortunately, one does not have to preclude the other. What is needed is an approach that combines the two in a complementary manner—a method that presents the two as mutually supportive and taught in a manner that makes the interrelationships clear to children. This approach can be achieved when phonics instruction is provided within the context of real reading tasks and texts, especially through the use of quality children's literature.

This article presents a means to teach phonics in conjunction with children's literature. First, I present an overview of the research. Second, I describe a comprehensive, instructional plan that unites phonics instruction and children's literature. Third, I discuss when and when not to use the strategy.

Phonics Rationale

Considerable research documents the importance of early, intensive phonics instruction so that children acquire independence in word identification (Chall, 1983; Johnson & Baumann, 1984; Pflaum, Walberg, Karegianes, & Rasher, 1980; Williams, 1985). According to Chall (1987), "Research evidence over the past 70 years indicates overwhelmingly that direct instruction in phonics is needed and contributes to better development of decoding, word recognition, and comprehension (p. 8). This same conclusion was drawn by the authors of *Becoming a Nation of Readers:* "On the average, children who are taught phonics get off to a better start in learning to read than children who are not taught phonics" (Anderson, Hiebert, Scott, & Wilkinson, 1985, p. 37). Thus, there is strong support for the value of phonics instruction.

Literature Rationale

In 1981, Koeller wrote an article for *The Reading Teacher* titled "25 Years Advocating Children's Literature in the Reading Program." Since then we have witnessed nothing less than an explosion of research and theory that supports the use of children's literature in reading instruction (e.g., Boehnlein, 1987; Eldredge & Butterfield, 1986; Holdaway, 1982; Tunnell & Jacobs, 1989). Research has shown that children absorb the language they hear and read, and, in time, use that language as part of their own (Cazden, 1972; Chomsky, 1972; White, 1984). Hence, "the richer the language environment, the richer the language learning" (Cullinan, 1987, p. 5).

The California English-Language Arts Framework (1987) called for a "literature-driven curriculum" an attempt to communicate culture through literature and cultivate lifelong readers (Smith, 1989). Thus, if we wish to stimulate the imagination, provide strong language models, expose students to lucid discourse, and expand their cultural awareness, we need quality, memorable literature in the reading program.

Combining Strengths

Combining the strengths of a literature-based and an explicit phonics perspective is endorsed by several writers. For example, Samuels (1988) and Winograd and Greenlee (1986) recommend a balanced reading program—one that combines decoding skills with the skills of reading in context.

Heymsfeld (1989) acknowledges the energy and excitement of whole language instruction but takes issue with whole language advocates' discarding of traditional skill-based instruction. She urges teachers to "use common sense and experience to create a combination program" (p. 68).

What constitutes a balanced or combined approach? Botel and Seaver (1984) recommend engaging children in the choral reading of a folk rhyme leading to sentence investigation, phonic investigation, and finally to mastery of consonant-vowel-consonant syllable patterns contained in the folk rhyme. The progression is whole-to-part.

Taking this concept a step further, I propose a whole-part-whole sequence, integrating phonics instruction with quality children's literature as follows:

1. *Whole*: Read, comprehend, and enjoy a whole, quality literature selection.

2. *Part*: Provide instruction in a high utility phonic element by drawing from or extending the preceding literature selection.

3. *Whole*: Apply the new phonic skill when reading (and enjoying) another whole, high quality literature selection.

Starting with a whole piece of literature reflects both common sense and sound pedagogy. Zeroing in on a targeted phonic element soon after it has been heard repeatedly in an enjoyable story contextualizes the decoding lesson—a welcome alternative to phonics-in-isolation. Practicing and applying a phonic principle in quality children's literature provides students familiar, meaningful, natural language and engrossing plots. Essentially, the whole-part-whole framework connects learning to pronounce words with real reading.

Sample Lesson

This lesson demonstrates how a first-grade teacher could use children's literature to teach short *a* to a group of children who have a demonstrated need for this skill. The lesson is structured according to the three-step, whole-part-whole format.

Step 1: Whole

The teacher reads aloud *Angus and the Cat* (Flack. 1931). In this listen/enjoy step, the teacher models expressive oral reading and promotes the enjoyment of an engaging tale. Extension activities for this step could include: student dramatization during teacher rereading, or comparing and contrasting this story with other cat/dog stories such as *Alex and the Cat* (Griffith, 1982).

Step 2: Part

In this step, the teacher provides instruction in short *a* by drawing from the preceding piece of literature. She begins with verbal explanation and teacher modeling by saying, "Today you will learn one sound that the letter *a* may stand for. This will help you read many more words that contain the letter *a*." Next, she prints on the chalkboard a portion of the story that contains examples of short *a* such as the following:

> *Angus missed the little CAT. But—at lunch time he heard this noise: PURRRRR—and there she was again. And Angus knew and the CAT knew that Angus knew that —Angus was GLAD the cat came back!*

The teacher reads the story excerpt, pausing and underlining the short *a* words (CAT, *at*, CAT, *that*, *that*, GLAD, *cat*, *back*) and then says. "The sound I hear when I come to each underlined letter *a* is /a/. Read this part of the story with me slowly and listen for the /a/ sound." The teacher and students can reread tile story excerpt several times until the students make the short *a* letter-sound association.

To enhance the short *a* letter-sound association, the teacher displays an apple and says, "You can remember the short *a* sound by thinking of this apple; /a/ is the first sound in apple. So, when you come to a word you cannot pronounce that has the letter *a* in it like *cat*, *that*, or *glad*, think of the sound at the beginning of apple, and see if this helps you say the word."

The teacher next moves to guided practice, which affords students the opportunity to exercise a new skill under teacher supervision. She does this by introducing a manipulative word slotter, which includes a stationary medial short *a* between movable beginning and ending consonants. Working with individual word slotters or an oversized group slotter, the teacher asks the students to construct specific words or has them experiment with generating real and nonsense words. Some children may find it easier to blend phonograms (word families) rather than individual letters. Therefore, an option would be to secure the final consonant strip with a paper clip, so the students could blend initial consonants with short *a* phonograms (*an*, *at*, *ad*, *ant*, etc.).

To provide guided practice of short *a* in larger language units, the teacher next introduces the sentence slotter that consists of three moveable strips. The first strip presents adjectives containing short *a*; the second contains two subordinating conjunctions; and the third includes several dependent clauses. Again working either with individual slotters or an oversized group slotter, the teacher has the students construct various plausible and silly sentences related to *Angus and the Cat* that contain examples of short *a* words. As an alternative, the teacher can leave the final strip blank, requiring the students to generate the sentence endings.

The slotter activity not only provides short *a* practice; it also teaches the function words *was*, *when*, and *because* through incidental learning (exposure and repetition). And it enables students to experience comfort and success with sophisticated sentences.

Step 3: Whole

The teacher presents a new book such as *Who Took The Farmer's Hat?* (Nodset, 1963) or *The Cat in the Hat* (Seuss, 1957) that contains examples of short *a* in context. The teacher has deliberately dovetailed the decoding skill with the application story so that children sense the connection. Capable readers may then read the story independently.

Less confident readers may benefit from choral reading of the application story in a big book format. Reading in unison from an enlarged text allows the less skilled readers to experience fluency (Tracht-enburg & Ferruggia, 1989). Another alternative is partner reading (Whisler, 1976): Working as a team, two students read aloud, alternating pages, and provide support for one another.

Regardless of the ability level, all students have the opportunity in Step 3 to apply the newly learned skill in a whole, rich, familiar context as they connect reading skill instruction with storybook reading.

The appendix contains a bibliography of trade books that can be used for teaching and applying short and long vowels.

When and When Not to Use This Strategy

Phonics instruction should aim to teach only the most important and regular sound-symbol relationships (Anderson et al., 1985). Even with meaning-enriched approaches such as whole-part-whole, teacher judgment must be exercised. The instructional progression detailed in this article should not be used for all phonic elements, with all children, or with all literature selections. Therefore, use the approach *selectively,* and only for high utility phonic elements or skills (e.g., see research on the frequency/utility of phonic generalizations by Bailey, 1967; Burmeister, 1968; Clymer, 1963; and Emans, 1967). Also, use the approach *discriminatingly,* that is, only with children who need such instruction. Diagnostic measures such as informal reading inventories and anecdotal records of students' oral reading will assist teachers in identifying which skills to teach to particular children. Setting up needs groups for skill instruction is more efficient and sensible than offering blanket instruction for all children, some of whom may already know what you are teaching.

Conclusion

There is empirical evidence for the value and importance of early, explicit instruction in phonic analysis. Likewise, there is evidence to document that students benefit by reading high quality children's books. Teaching phonics in association with children's literature maximizes learning opportunities for beginning readers. The whole-part-whole instructional framework integrates learning to read with real reading, and its objective is to produce learners who not only *can* read but who also *choose* to read for pleasure and self-satisfaction.

References

Anderson, R C., Hiebert, E.H., Scott, J.A., & Wilkinson, I.A.G. (1985). *Becoming a nation of readers: The report of The Commission on Reading.* Washington, DC: National Institute of Education.

Baily, M.H. (1967). The utility of phonic generalizations in grades one through six. *The Reading Teacher, 20,* 413–418.

Boehnlein, M. (1987). Reading intervention for high risk first graders. *Educational Leadership, 44*(6), 32–37.

Botel, M. & Seaver, J.T. (1984). *Phonics revisited: Toward an integrated methodology.* Paper presented at the annual meeting of the Keystone State Reading Association, Hershey, PA.

Burmeister, L.E. (1968). Usefulness of phonic generalizations. *The Reading Teacher, 21,* 349–356.

Calfee, R., & Drum. P. (1968). Research on teaching reading. In M.C. Wittrock (Ed.), *Handbook of research on teaching* (pp. 804–849). New York: Macmillan.

California State Department of Education. (1987). *English-language arts framework.* Sacramento, CA: California State Department of Education.

Cazden, C . (1972). *Child language and education.* New York: Holt.

Chall, J. (1983). *Learning to read: The great debate.* New York: McGraw-Hill.

Chall, J. (1987). Reading and early childhood education: The critical issues. *Principal, 66*(5), 6–9.

Chomsky, C. (1972). Stages in language development and reading exposure. *Harvard Educational Review, 42,* 1–33.

Clymer, T. (1963). The utility of phonic generalizations in the primary grades. *The Reading Teacher, 16,* 252–258.

Culinan, B.E. (Ed.). (1987). *Children's literature in the reading program.* Newark, DE: International Reading Association.

Eldredge, J.L., & Butterfield, D. (1986). Alternatives to traditional reading instruction. *The Reading Teacher, 40,* 32–37.

Emans, R. (1967). The usefulness of phonic generalizations above the primary grades. *The Reading Teacher, 20,* 419–425.

Flack, M. (1931). *Angus and the cat.* New York: Doubleday.

Griffith, H.V. (1982). *Alex and the cat.* New York: Greenwillow.

Heymsfeld, C.R. (1989). Filling the hole in whole language. *Educational Leadership, 46*(6), 65–68.

Holdaway, D. (1982). Shared book experience: Teaching reading using favorite books. *Theory into Practice,* 21, 293–300.

Hoskisson, K. (1975), The many facets of assisted reading. *Elementary English, 52,* 312–315.

Johnson, D.D., & Baumann, J.F. (1984). Word identification. In P. David Pearson (Ed.), *Handbook of reading research* (pp. 583–608). New York: Longman.

Koeller, S. (1981). Twenty-five years advocating children's literature in the reading program. *The Reading Teacher, 34,* 552–556.

Nodsel, J.L., (1963). *Who took the farmer's hat?* New York: Harper & Row.

Plfaum, S.W., Walberg, H., Karegianes, M.L., & Rasher, P. (1980). Reading Instruction: A quantitative analysis. *Educational Researcher, 9*(7), 12–18.

Samuels, S.J. (1988). Decoding and automataicity: Helping poor readers become automatic at word recognition. *The Reading Teacher, 41,* 756–760.

Seuss, Dr. (1957). *The cat in the hat.* New York: Random House.

Smith, C.B. (1989). Trends in teaching reading. *The Reading Teacher, 42,* 720.

Trachtenburg, P., & Ferruggia, A. (1989). Big books from little voices: Reaching high risk beginning readers. *The Reading Teacher, 42,* 284–289.

Tunnell, M.O., & Jacobs, J.S. (1989). Using "real" books: Research findings on literature based reading instruction. *The Reading Teacher, 42,* 470–477.

Whisler, N.G. (1976). Pupil partners: Strategy for oral reading practice. *Language Arts, 53,* 387–389.

White, D. (1984). *Books before five.* Portsmouth, NH: Heinemann.

Williams, J.P. (1985). The case for explicit decoding instruction. In J. Osborn, P.T. Wilson, & R.C. Anderson (Eds.), *Reading education: Foundations for a literate America* (pp. 205–213). Lexington, MA: Lexington Books.

Winograd, P., & Greenlee, M. (1986). Students need a balanced reading program. *Educational Leadership, 43*(7), 16–21.

Appendix

Trade Books That Repeat Phonic Elements

Short a

Flack, Marjorie. *Angus and the Cat.* Doubleday, 1931.
Griffith, Helen. *Alex and the Cat.* Greenwillow, 1982.
Kent, Jack. *The Fat Cat.* Scholastic, 1971.
Most, Bernard. *There's an Ant in Anthony.* William Morrow, 1980.
Nodset, Joan. *Who Took the Farmer's Hat?* Harper & Row, 1963.
Robins, Joan. *Addie Meets Max.* Harper & Row, 1985.
Schmidt, Karen. *The Gingerbread Man.* Scholastic, 1985.
Seuss, Dr. *The Cat in the Hat.* Random House, 1957.

Long a

Aardema, Verna. *Bringing the Rain to Kapiti Plain.* Dial, 1981.
Bang, Molly. *The Paper Crane.* Greenwillow, 1985.
Blume, Judy. *The Pain and the Great One.* Bradbury, 1974.

Byars, Betsy. *The Lace Snail.* Viking, 1975.
Henkes, Kevin. *Sheila Rae, The Brave.* Greenwillow, 1987.
Hines, Anna G. *Taste the Raindrops.* Greenwillow, 1983.

Short and Long a

Aliki. *Jack and Jake.* Greenwillow, 1986.
Slobodkina, Esphyr. *Caps for Sale.* Addison-Wesley, 1940.

Short e

Ets, Marie Hall. *Elephant in a Well.* Viking, 1972.
Galdone, Paul. *The Little Red Hen.* Scholastic, 1973.
Ness, Evaline. *Yeck Eck.* E. P Dutton, 1974.
Shecter, Ben. *Hester the Jester.* Harper & Row, 1977.
Thayer, Jane. *I Don't Believe in Elves.* William Morrow, 1975.
Wing, Henry Ritchet. *Ten Pennies for Candy.* Holt, Rinehart & Winston, 1963.

Long e

Galdone, Paul. *Little Bo-Peep.* Clarion/Ticknor & Fields, 1986.
Keller, Holly. *Ten Sleepy Sheep.* Greenwillow, 1983.
Martin, Bill. *Brown Bear, Brown Bear. What Do You See?* Henry Holt, 1967.
Oppenheim, Joanne. *Have You Seen Trees?* Young Scott Books, 1967.
Soule, Jean C. *Never Tease a Weasel.* Parents' Magazine Press, 1964.
Thomas, Patricia. *"Stand Back," said the Elephant, "I'm Going to Sneeze!* Lothrop, Lee & Shepard, 1971.

Short i

Browne, Anthony. *Willy the Wimp.* Alfred A. Knopf, 1984.
Ets, Marie Hall. *Gilberto and the Wind.* Viking, 1966.
Hutchins. Pat. *Titch.* Macmillan, 1971.
Keats, Ezra Jack. *Whistle for Willie.* Viking, 1964.
Lewis, Thomas P. *Call for Mr. Sniff.* Harper & Row. 1981.
Lobel, Arnold. *Small Pig.* Harper & Row, 1969.
McPhail, David. *Fix-it.* E.P Dutton, 1984.
Patrick, Gloria. *This Is...* Carolrhoda, 1970.
Robins, Joan. *My Brother, Will.* Greenwillow, 1986.

Long i

Berenstain, Stan and Jan. *The Bike Lesson.* Random House, 1964.
Cameron, John. *If Mice Could Fly.* Atheneum, 1979.
Cole, Sheila. *When the Tide Is Low.* Lothrop, Lee & Shepard, 1985.
Gelman. Rita. *Why Can't I Fly?* Scholastic, 1976.
Hazen, Barbara S. *Tight Times.* Viking, 1979.

Short o

Benchley, Nathaniel. *Oscar Otter.* Harper & Row, 1966.
Dunrea, Olivier. *Mogwogs on the March!* Holiday House, 1985.
Emberley, Barbara, *Drummer Hoff.* Prentice-Hall, 1967.
McKissack, Patricia C. *Flossie & the Fox.* Dial, 1986.
Miller, Patricia, and Iran Seligman. *Big Frogs, Little Frogs.* Holt, Rinehart & Winston, 1963.

Rice, Eve. "The Frog and the Ox" from *Once in a Wood*. Greenwillow, 1979.
Seuss, Dr. *Fox in Socks*. Random House, 1965.

Long o

Cole, Brock. *The Giant's Toe*. Farrar, Straus. & Giroux, 1986.
Gerstein, Mordicai. *Roll Over!* Crown, 1984.
Johnston, Tony. *The Adventures of Mole and Troll*. G.P. Putnam's Sons, 1972.
Johnston, Tony. *Night Noises and Other Mole and Troll Stories*. G.P. Putnam's Sons, 1977.
Shulevitz. Uri. *One Monday Morning*. Charles Scribner's Sons, 1967.
Tresselt, Alvin. *White Snow, Bright Snow*. Lothrop, Lee & Shepard, 1947.

Short u

Carroll, Ruth. *Where's the Bunny?* Henry Z. Walck, 1950.
Cooney, Nancy E. *Donald Says Thumbs Down*. G. P. Putnam's Sons, 1987.
Friskey, Margaret. *Seven Little Ducks*. Children's Press, 1940.
Lorenz, Lee: *Big Gus and Little Gus*. Prentice-Hall, 1982.
Marshall, James. *The Cut-Ups*. Viking Kestrel, 1984.
Udry, Janice May. *Thump and Plunk*. Harper & Row, 1981.
Yashima, Taro. Umbrella. Viking Penguin, 1958.

Long u

Lobel, Anita. *The Troll Music*. Harper & Row, 1966.
Segal, Lore. Tell *Me a Trudy*. Farrar, Straus, & Giroux, 1977.
Slobodkin, Louis. *"Excuse Me—Certainly!"* Vanguard Press, 1959.

Literacy Vignette: The Second Draft

Arlene R.H. Pincus

It is Monday morning in a third-grade classroom in Maplewood, New Jersey, where the building principal is modeling writing conferences for a new teacher. The principal bends close to Christine. "What have you been writing about?" she asks.

"I started over writing about my kitten," Christine announces. "I threw out my first draft."

"I'd really like to see both," the principal prompts. "Can you show me the first draft, too?"

Christine complies by spreading out a crumpled paper retrieved from the wastebasket. The principal studies the two stories. "You're right," she agrees. "This second one is much more interesting. What happened to make you change your story?"

"Simple!" Christine explains. "I wrote the first draft Friday. We got our kittens Saturday. I didn't know anything about cats on Friday!"

Source: Pincus, Arlene, R.H. 1990. *The Reading Teacher* (May):654.

CHAPTER NINE

READING COMPREHENSION

Schema Theory

Schema theory is a way of trying to explain how people store knowledge in their minds, how they use the knowledge they have, and how they acquire new knowledge. This theory has the fundamental assumption that spoken or written text does not in itself carry meaning. Rather, a text simply provides directions for listeners or readers as to how they should construct the intended meaning using their own, previously acquired knowledge. This **does not** mean that one does not learn from text. Rather, the information a reader possesses **interacts** with the new or slightly modified information presented in the text.

Terminology

Schema—The way knowledge is organized or structured by the mind (Rumelhart, 1981). Roughly, it is a *concept*.

Schemata—the plural of schema. They are the internal, informal explanations about the nature of events, objects, or situations each individual faces. It can be considered to be a *network of concepts*. Schemata are characterized as active (changing) processes representing knowledge.

Brief Basic Principles

1. Each schema is incomplete—bits of information are missing. Schema theorists visualize missing information as empty slots waiting to be filled—perhaps by written discourse. When a reader reads, the information in the head (schemata) interacts with information on the page to **assimilate** new information to be slotted.

2. When a reader reads about a totally new concept, he or she must create a new schema (**accommodation**). This is a very difficult task to do!

3. When a reader reads text that contradicts past schematic information, the reader may modify an existing schema to **accommodate** this new information.

Schema Theory and the Four Aspects of Reading

Reading as an Active Search for Meaning

1. Reading is not "sounding out" nor is it simply pronouncing words. Reading is a **meaning getting** activity.

2. Reading is not simply recalling what has been read. Johnston (1983) has written:

   We do not consider readers to have comprehended something if they can give only a rote recall of the elements. We consider that readers have comprehended a text only when they have established logical connections among the ideas in the text and can express these in an alternate form. In this way, inferences are critical acts of comprehension, since they allow us to make various words meaningful, join together propositions and sentences, and fill in the missing chunks of information.

3. Read this **surface structure**: "Billy hesitantly handed his work in to his teacher."

   What might you **infer** about the **deep structure**?

Reading as a Constructive Process

1. Reading is a **constructive process** during which the reader makes meaningful connections among ideas in a text and to background knowledge.

2. Langer (1982) has written:

   *Comprehension is not a simple text-based process in which readers piece together what the words, sentences, or paragraphs "say"—as if words themselves have some inherent meaning. Nor is it simply a concept-driven process in which readers begin with a global notion of what the text will be about, and anticipate the larger meanings the text will convey. Rather, comprehension is a process which requires **readers**—real live readers with ideas and attitudes of their own—to interpret what the author is saying.*

3. Place a piece of paper over the text below so that you will be able to read it just one sentence at a time. After you look at the first sentence, jot down what you think the text is about. Do the same for the second and third sentences combining information as you read.

   TEXT:

   He asked her for her name.

   She was hesitant, but decided to give it to him.

   He then asked her to show her driver's license as the red and blue lights flashed in her rear view mirror.

---

4. What you have been doing during this process is called **hypothesis testing**. You are constructing a mental model of the text as you are reading. You revise this model as you continue your reading.

Reading as an Application of Different Kinds of Knowledge

1. To a great extent, a reader relies upon information already in his or her mind. This information will shape his or her interpretation of what is happening in text.

2. Read the following text:

   Mike could see the improvement he was making. His mentor was absolutely correct: Practice was making a significant contribution to his once amateur abilities. He only hoped that his rapid progress would continue.

   (What is the above about?_____)

3. Langer (1982) maintained that background knowledge can affect comprehension in at least four different ways:

   A. By influencing the way information is organized and stored in memory.
   B. By influencing the type of information brought to mind when reading about a topic.
   C. By influencing the associations made, due to personal experiences and background knowledge.
   D. By influencing the language or vocabulary applied because of the perspective brought to the task of reading.

4. Two things teachers need to keep in mind:

   A. Children cannot be expected to read with comprehension if they have no way of connecting the new information in the text to their background knowledge.
   B. Since no two readers will have had the same life experiences, teachers should expect differences in they ways students interpret text.

Reading as a Strategic Process

1. We adjust our reading behaviors contingent upon our purposes.

2. How are your reading behaviors different when reading the following materials:

   A. Newspaper
   B. College textbook upon which you will be tested.
   C. A romance novel or Louis Lamour book.
   D. *Newsweek*
   E. *War and Peace*
   F. A Silver Burdett & Ginn Manual
   G. Instructions to putting together a child's new kitchenette Christmas gift.

3. Unlike beginning readers, adept readers are aware of what they are doing as they read, and of what they need to do to meet their purposes. Awareness of one's own mental activity is referred to as **metacognition**.

Metacognition

Definition: Metacognition refers to the knowledge and control which students have over their own thinking and learning activities.

Metacognition in reading refers to three things:

1. **Self-knowledge.** When readers are aware of self in relation to tests and tasks, they are in a better position to use reading strategies effectively.

   A. Do children know what reading is for?
   B. Do they know what the reader's role is?
   C. Do they know their options?
   D. Are they aware of their strengths as readers and learners?
   E. Do they recognize that some texts are harder than others because of their personal knowledge?

2. **Task-knowledge.** Experienced readers are strategic readers. They use their task knowledge to meet the demands inherent in difficult texts. For example, they know how to analyze a reading task, reflect on what they know or don't know about the text to be read, establish purposes and plans for reading, and evaluate their progress in light of purposes for reading. How they read a newspaper will be quite different from how they read a novel.

3. **Self-monitoring.** As we read we monitor our reading progress contingent upon whether or not what we are reading makes sense. This device might be called a *metacognitive sensor.* Fluent reading might be interrupted by this sensor when what we read doesn't make sense.

Where comprehension can break down:

1. Failure to understand a word

   A. Novel word
   B. Known word that doesn't make sense in the context

2. Failure to understand a sentence

   A. Can find no interpretation
   B. Can find only a vague, abstract interpretation
   C. Can find several possible interpretations
   D. Interpretation conflicts with prior knowledge

3. Failure to understand how one sentence relates to another

   A. Interpretation of one sentence conflicts with another
   B. Can find no connection between the sentences
   C. Can find several possible connections between the sentences

4. Failure to understand how the whole text fits together

    A. Can find no point to the whole or part of the text
    B. Cannot understand why certain episodes or sections occurred
    C. Cannot understand the motivations of certain characters

Possible remedies for comprehension breakdowns:

1. Ignore and read on, because this information is relatively unimportant.

2. Suspend judgment because it is likely to be cleared up later.

3. Form a tentative hypothesis to be tested as reading continues.

4. Reread the current sentence(s) or look for a tentative hypothesis.

5. Reread the previous context to resolve the contradiction.

6. Go to an expert source, because it simply doesn't make sense.

General metacognitive teaching suggestions:

1. For content area assignments, let students know the extent to which they should monitor their comprehension. Must is all make sense right away? Should they just try to get the flavor and wait for class to get their questions answered?

2. Always focus on meaning when teaching reading. Use activities that make sense to the students. Use materials that they can understand.

3. Encourage an active approach toward learning by encouraging students to ask questions whenever they do not understand something in class or in their assignments.

4. Try to overcome the students' learned helplessness. Provide situations in which additional effort can make a difference.

5. Teach students that taking risks and making guesses is good. This is an effective strategy in many cases of comprehension breakdown.

6. Teach the students that comprehension can break down at one of four levels: word, sentence, paragraph, or passage. Tell them that the first step is to identify the level in which it occurs.

7. Use explaining and modeling to teach the taxonomy of remedies for comprehension failures. Help students use it when they let you know they are having problems with comprehension.

8. Whenever students come to class with reports of comprehension problems ("I didn't understand it!"), you have an opportunity to teach comprehension monitoring. Don't explain the material to them. Instead, help them remedy the situation by applying strategies.

The Oral Recitation Lesson

Purpose: To develop reading fluency and comprehension abilities in elementary school students.

Procedures:

Day 1

Reading/Presentation Phase

1. Teacher introduces story with an emphasis on title and setting. Children make predictions about the story.

2. Teacher reads the story expressively to students. Students follow along in their own copy of the story.

3. Children respond to story upon completion.

4. Discussion of elements of story structure: Setting, characters, goals, problem/conflict, and resolution.

5. Teacher summarizes the story (modeling).

6. New vocabulary words are introduced.

Rehearsal/Practice Phase

1. Teacher reviews the story while children assist.

2. Teacher reminds students that what they are doing would assist them in reading with expression.

3. Teacher reads the first page of the story again to the children. Discussion of language fluency, stress, and stops ensues.

4. Choral reading of first page.

5. Each ensuing page is modeled by the teacher followed by choral reading until the story is completed.

Adapted from Reutzel, D.R. & Hollingsworth, P.M. (1993). Effects of fluency training on second graders' reading comprehension. *Journal of Educational Research*, Vol 86 (6). pp. 325–331.

Day 2

Performance/Recitation Phase

1. Children are instructed that they will form reading partners and take turns reading the story.

2. Teacher reminds students about what makes fluent reading *fluent reading*! (Language flows, contains stress, and contains stops.)

3. Teacher models reading the first page.

4. Partner reading ensues until the story is completed.

Semantic Mapping

1. Write the name of the topic about which the children will be reading on the chalkboard, an overhead, or chart paper.

2. Encourage the children to brainstorm words pertaining to the topic. Write these words in list form on a separate recording surface.

3. Have the children categorize the words.

4. Return to the semantic map and label the categories and list the specifics in branches from the categories.

5. Repeat this procedure after children have read about the topic or have completed a unit on the topic.

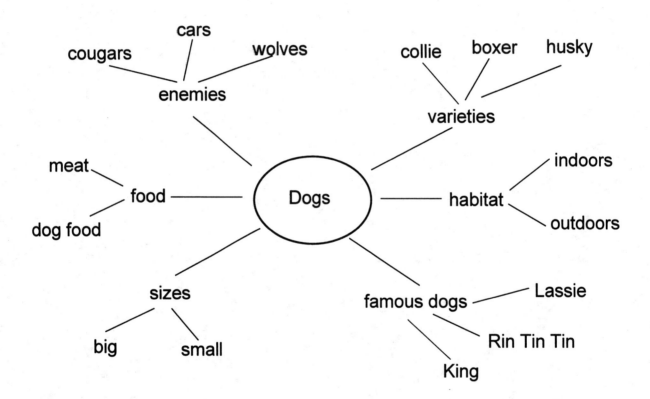

Semantic Mapping with a Story

Goals

Semantic mapping with children's literature helps students understand important characteristics of a story, increases their appreciation of literature, and improves their reading and writing competencies.

Procedures

1. The teacher introduces the literary elements of setting, characterization, plot development, conflict, theme, episodes, emotions, and moods/tones.

2. The teacher draws simple maps of stories of which the children are familiar (e.g., "The Three Billy Goats").

3. The teacher reads a story to the children. The children note elements of the setting, characters, etc.

4. A new map is made with the children contributing the characteristics noted during the reading.

5. Children use semantic mapping as a follow-up activity after reading stories.

6. Children reading the same book/story should share their own maps with peers to see similarities and differences in interpretations.

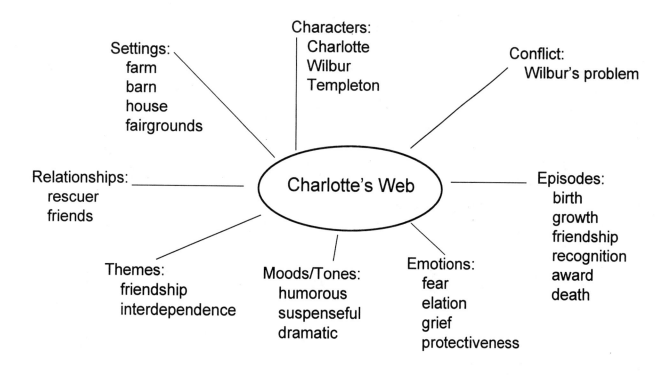

Compare/Contrast Chart
(Venn Diagram)

Different   Alike   Different

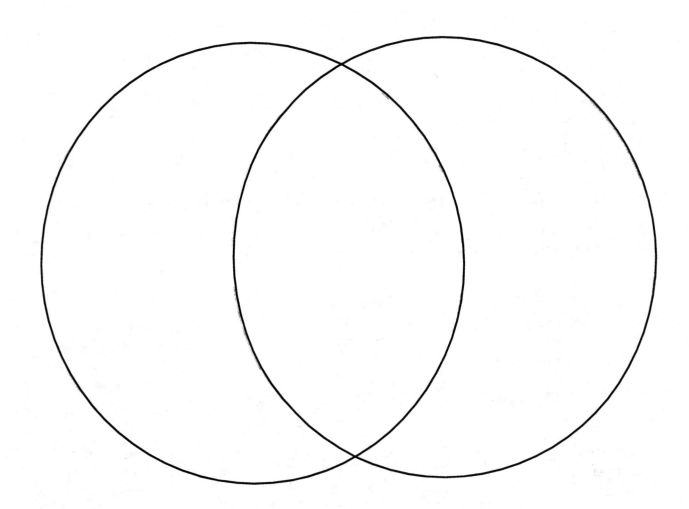

K-W-L-S

What I Already Know	What I Want to Know	What I Learned	What I Still Need to Know

Source: Sippola, Arne. 1990. *The Reading Teacher*, (March).

What's Next?
(A Lesson in Using Inference)

1. After eating breakfast, Joanne picked up her books, grabbed her lunch, and went to wait at the corner.

2. John looked out the window, put on his coat, picked up the snow shovel, and went outside.

3. After glancing at her watch, Joan picked up her pocketbook and ran out the door.

4. My mother baked a cake for us today. She wasn't there when we got home from school.

5. We returned home after school, hungry from a long day's work.

Where Is This Happening?
(A Lesson in Using Inference)

1. She looked up, her breathing apparatus heavy on her back, and watched the shark slowly swim by.

2. The desks were in order, the pencils sharpened, the chalkboard ready for another year.

3. The fumes of the trains, the stale air of the tunnel, and the rushing crowds gave her a headache.

4. As he glanced at the valley below, fear gripped him and he clung more closely to the ledge.

5. It was ten o'clock. The stores were closing, so there was a crowd as the people began to walk outside to their parked cars.

Story Map

Main Character(s):

Setting (Time and Place):

The Problem (or Source of Conflict):

The Steps Through Which the Problem Is Solved

    1.

    2.

    3.

The Way the Problem Is Finally Solved:

The Main Idea Told Throughout the Story:

The Title of the Story:

Story Frame

A good way to sum up the reading done is to put the story into a story frame. A story frame introduces the notion of characters, setting, and plot.

Divide the story into three separate sections so students get the idea of beginning, middle, and end. To do this, simply decide where the story naturally divides itself and give students the appropriate page numbers. Once they have experienced the concept of the story frame, they can become involved in choosing the three sections of the story as a group. This involvement is exceptionally beneficial for in-depth comprehension and such subtleties as character motivation, changes in setting, and plot development.

Story Frame: Characters, Setting, & Plot

CHARACTERS	SETTING	PLOT

Barrett's Taxonomy

1.0 Literal Recognition or Recall

    1.1 Recognition or recall of details
    1.2 Recognition or recall of main ideas
    1.3 Recognition or recall of sequence
    1.4 Recognition or recall of comparisons
    1.5 Recognition or recall of cause and effect relationships
    1.6 Recognition or recall of character traits

2.0 Inference

    2.1 Inferring supporting details
    2.2 Inferring the main idea
    2.3 Inferring sequence
    2.4 Inferring comparisons
    2.5 Inferring cause and effect relationships
    2.6 Inferring character traits
    2.7 Inferring outcomes
    2.8 Inferring about figurative language

3.0 Evaluation

    3.1 Judgments of reality or fantasy
    3.2 Judgments of fact or opinion
    3.3 Judgments of adequacy or validity
    3.4 Judgments of appropriateness
    3.5 Judgments of worth, desirability, or acceptability

4.0 Appreciation

    4.1 Emotional response to plot or theme
    4.2 Identification with characters and incidents
    4.3 Reactions to the author's use of language
    4.4 Imagery

The Scientist

There was a science professor at WSU who was experimenting with the hearing of frogs. He cut off one leg and told the frog to jump. It did. He cut off a second leg and told him to jump again. He did. The scientist cut off the third leg and told the frog to jump again. He did. The scientist then cut off the fourth leg and again commanded the frog to jump. This time the frog did not jump. The scientist concluded that when you cut off all four legs on a frog he loses his hearing.

1.1 With what animal was the scientist experimenting?

1.3 What was the second thing the scientist did in the story?

2.2 What is the author trying to tell you about this scientist?

2.5 What was the read reason the frog could not jump at the end of the story?

3.1 Do you think this experiment could really take place? Why/why not?

3.3 Do you think the scientist's experiment was valid? Why/why not?

4.1 Did you enjoy the author's intended humor? Why/why not?

4.4 Did you like the imagery created by the author? Why/why not?

Reading Comprehension: What Works (A Summary of Fielding/Pearson Research Synthesis)

1. Children should spend large amounts of time for real reading.

2. Teachers should provide teacher-directed instruction in comprehension *strategies*. (Metacognition) Durkin's research on teachers not teaching comprehension, but simply assessing comprehension abilities led to this redressing. *Explicit instruction* is beneficial to readers. This involves four phases: "teacher modeling and explanation of the strategy, guided practice during which teachers gradually give students more responsibility for task completion, independent practice accompanied by feedback, and application of the strategy in real reading situations."

3. Provide children opportunities for *choice*.

4. Assist children in selecting books that are "just right"—not to difficult and not too easy.

5. Allow and encourage students to reread textual material. Rereading has been shown to facilitate speed of reading, accuracy, phrasing, intonation, and general comprehension abilities.

6. Provide time for children to share their interpretations of books read. Reading is not just a cognitive experience, but a social one as well. This aspect facilitates a reader's ability to use inference. Cooperative learning groups are advocated.

7. We need less "teacher talk" and more opportunities for students to interact when discussing a literature reading.

8. Accept personal interpretations and reactions to literature. This is *inference*!

9. Use multiple approaches to teaching reading. . .!

Reading Comprehension: What Works

Perhaps the most sweeping changes in reading instruction in the last 15 years are in the area of comprehension. Once thought of as the natural result of decoding plus oral language, comprehension is now viewed as a much more complex process involving knowledge, experience, thinking, and teaching. It depends heavily on knowledge—both about the world at large and the worlds of language and print. Comprehension inherently involves inferential and evaluative thinking, not just literal reproduction of the author's words. Most important, it can be taught directly.

Two years ago we reviewed the most recent research about comprehension instruction (Pearson and Fielding 1991). Here, we revisit that research, supplementing it with current thinking about reading instruction, and transform the most consistent findings into practical guidelines for teachers.

We contend that a successful program of comprehension instruction should include four components:

- large amounts of time for actual text reading,

- teacher-directed instruction in comprehension strategies,

- opportunities for peer and collaborative learning, and

- occasions for students to talk to a teacher and one another about their responses to reading.

A program with these components will set the stage for students to be interested in and to succeed at reading—providing them the intrinsic motivation for continual learning.

Ample Time for Text Reading

One of the most surprising findings of classroom research of the 1970s and '80s was the small amount of time that children spent actually reading texts. Estimates ranged from 7 to 15 minutes per day from the primary to the intermediate grades (Anderson et al. 1985). Children typically spent more time working on reading skills via workbook-type assignments than putting these skills to work in reading connected texts. The skill time/reading time ratio was typically the highest for children of the lowest reading ability (Allington 1983b). Allocating ample time for actual text reading and ensuring that students are actually engaged in text reading during that time are among teachers' most important tasks in comprehension instruction.

Why is time for text reading important? The first benefit of time for reading is the sheer opportunity to orchestrate the skills and strategies that are important to proficient reading—including comprehension, As in sports and music, *practice makes perfect* in reading, too.

Second, reading results in *the acquisition of new knowledge,* which, in turn, fuels the comprehension process. Research of the late 1970s and early '80s consistently revealed a strong reciprocal relationship between prior knowledge and reading comprehension ability. The more one already knows, the more one comprehends; and the more one comprehends, the more one learns new knowledge to enable comprehension of an even greater and broader array of topics and texts.

Fielding, L., Pearson, D. (1994). "Reading Comprehension: What Works." *Educational Leadership,* 51, 5: 62-68. Reprinted with permission of the Association for Supervision and Curriculum Development. Copyright © 1994 by ASCD. All rights reserved.

The first part of this reciprocal relationship was the focus of much research of the last 15 years—developing methods for activating and adding to readers' knowledge base before reading to increase text understanding (Beck et al. 1982, Hansen and Pearson 1983). More recently, researchers have emphasized the second part of the relationship: the role that actual text reading plays in building knowledge. For example, increases in vocabulary and concept knowledge from reading silently (Nagy et al. 1987, Stallman 1991) and from being read to (Elley 1989) have been documented. Further, the positive statistical relationship between amount of time spent reading and reading comprehension (Anderson et al. 1988) may be largely attributable to the knowledge base that grows through text reading.

Recent research has debunked the misconception that only already-able readers can benefit from time spent in actual text reading, while less able readers should spend time on isolated skills instruction and workbook practice (Anderson et al. 1988, Leinhardt et al. 1981). A newer, more compelling argument is that the differing amounts of time teachers give students to read texts accounts for the widening gaps between more able and less able readers throughout the school grades (Allington 1983b, Stanovich 1986).

How much time should be devoted to actual text reading? At present research offers no answers, but we recommend that, of the time set aside for reading instruction, students should have more time to read than the combined total allocated for *learning* about reading and *talking or writing* about what has been read.

Getting the Most Out of Reading Time

The equivocal results of sustained silent reading programs throughout the years (Manning and Manning 1984) suggest, though, that simply allocating time is not enough. Teachers can increase the likelihood that more time for contextual reading will translate into improved comprehension skills in the following ways.

1. *Choice.* Teachers can give children opportunities and guidance in making text selections. Although we know of no research that directly links choice to reading comprehension growth, we speculate that choice is related to interest and motivation, both of which are related directly to learning (Anderson et al. 1987).

2. *Optimal difficulty.* Teachers can monitor students' and their own selections to ensure that all students spend most of their time reading books that are appropriate in difficulty-not so hard that a student's cognitive resources are occupied with just figuring out how to pronounce the words and not so easy that nothing new is likely to be learned.

3. *Multiple readings.* Teachers can honor and encourage rereading of texts, which research suggests leads to greater fluency and comprehension (Allington 1983a). Although most research about repeated reading of passages has focused on improvements in reading speed, accuracy, phrasing, and intonation, a growing number of studies have documented improved comprehension as well (Dowhower 1987).

4. *Negotiating meaning socially.* "Silent" reading time shouldn't be entirely silent. Teachers can (a) allow part of the time for reading in pairs, including pairs of different abilities and ages (Koskinen and Blum 1986, Labbo and Teale 1990); and (b) provide regular opportunities for readers to discuss their reading with the teacher and with one another. We view reading comprehension as a social as well as a cognitive process. Conversation not only raises the status of independent silent reading from a time filler to an important part of the reading program; it also gives students another opportunity to practice and build comprehension skills collaboratively, a topic to which we return below. Atwell (1987) and Hansen

1(1987) further argue that these conversations help to build the all-important community of readers that is the essence of literature-based programs.

Teacher-Directed Instruction

Research from the 1980s indicated that in traditional reading classrooms. time for comprehension instruction was as rare as time for actual text reading. After extensive observations in intermediate-grade classrooms, Durkin (1978-1979) concluded that teachers were spending very little time on actual comprehension instruction. Although they gave many workbook assignments and asked many questions about text content, Durkin judged that these exercises mostly tested students' understanding instead of teaching them how to comprehend.

In response to Durkin's findings, much research in the 1980s was devoted to discovering how to teach comprehension strategies directly. In the typical study of this type, readers were directly taught how to perform a strategy that skilled readers used during reading. Then, their abilities both in strategy use and text comprehension were compared either to their own performance before instruction or to the performance of similar readers who were not taught the strategy directly. *Explicit instruction,* the name given to one such widely researched model, involves four phases: teacher modeling and explanation of a strategy, guided practice during which teachers gradually give students more responsibility for task completion, independent practice accompanied by feedback, and application of the strategy in real reading situations (Pearson and Dole 1987).

In one of the biggest success stories of the time period, research showed repeatedly that comprehension can in fact be taught. Many strategies have been taught successfully:

- using background knowledge to make inferences (Hansen and Pearson 1983) or set purposes (Ogle 1986);

- getting the main idea (Baumann 1984);

- identifying the sources of information needed to answer a question (Raphael and Pearson 1985); and using the typical structure of stories (Fitzgerald and Spiegel 1983) or expository texts (Armbruster et al. 1987) to help students understand what they are reading.

One of the most exciting results of this body of research was that comprehension strategy instruction is especially effective for students who began the study as poor comprehenders—probably because they are less likely to invent effective strategies on their own. In some studies, less able readers who had been taught a comprehension strategy were indistinguishable from more able readers who had not been taught the strategy directly.

After more than a decade of research and criticism from both sides of the controversy about comprehension strategy instruction, we have a much clearer understanding of what quality instruction looks like and how to make it part of a larger comprehension instructional program.

Authenticity of strategies. First, the strategies students are taught should be as much as possible like the ones actual readers use when they comprehend successfully. To meet this criterion of authentic use, instruction should focus on the flexible application of the strategy rather than a rigid sequence of steps. It should also externalize the thinking processes of skilled readers—not create artificial processes that apply only to contrived instructional or assessment situations.

Demonstration. Teachers should also demonstrate how to apply each strategy successfully—what it is, how it is carried out, and when and why it should be used (Duffy et al. 1988, Paris et al. 1991). Instead of just talking about a strategy, teachers need to illustrate the processes they use by thinking aloud, or modeling mental processes, while they read.

Guided practice. A phase in which teachers and students practice the strategy together is critical to strategy learning, especially for less-successful comprehenders. During this time teachers can give feedback about students' attempts and gradually give students more and more responsibility for performing the strategy and evaluating their own performance (Pearson and Dole 1987). This is also the time when students can hear about one another's reasoning processes—another activity especially important for less strategic readers.

Authenticity of texts. Finally, students must be taught, reminded, and given time to practice comprehension strategies while reading everyday texts—not just specially constructed materials or short workbook passages. We would like to see real texts used more and earlier in comprehension strategy instruction. Using real texts, we believe, will increase the likelihood that students will transfer the use of taught strategies to their independent reading—and that, after all, is the ultimate goal of instruction.

Opportunities for Peer and Collaborative Learning

We are becoming more and more aware of the social aspects of instruction and their influence on cognitive outcomes. In addition to equity and the sense of community fostered through peer and collaborative learning, students gain access to one another's thinking processes.

Perhaps the most widely researched peer learning model is *cooperative learning.* This approach has been examined in a variety of academic disciplines (Johnson and Johnson 1985, Slavin 1987)—with the focus in a few cases on literacy learning, including comprehension (Meloth 1991, Stevens et al. 1987). A synthesis of this research suggests that cooperative learning is most effective when students clearly understand the teacher's goals, when goals are group oriented and the criterion of success is satisfactory learning by each group member, when students are expected and taught to explain things to one another instead of just providing answers, and when group activities supplement rather than supplant teacher-directed instruction. At its best, cooperative learning has positive social and cognitive benefits for students of all abilities.

Other models of peer teaching also have been investigated—for example, *reciprocal teaching.* In this model, students take turns leading dialogues that involve summarizing, asking an important question about what was read, predicting information, and attempting to clarify confusions. Reciprocal teaching is effective when students, not just teachers, teach their peers to engage in these dialogues (Palincsar et al. 1987).

Time to Talk about Reading

Some form of discussion or explication of a text has been a feature of reading classrooms for years, but traditional teacher-student discussions have been consistently criticized because they emphasize teacher control and learning a single interpretation. Critics have tended to advocate student-centered discussions that honor multiple interpretations. Cazden (1986) and many others noted a universal format of traditional teacher student discussions, called the IRE format. The teacher *initiates* a question, a student *responds,* and the teacher *evaluates* the response before moving to another question.

Recently, various forms of teacher student discussions have been geared toward achieving the following three goals.

1. *Changing teacher-student interaction patterns.*
   In the traditional recitation format, teachers choose the topics and, through feedback to students, control which student answers are viewed as correct and incorrect. One outcome

---

119

of the recitation format is that teachers talk a lot! Typically, teachers talk as much as or more than all students combined, because their questions and feedback focus on transmitting the text interpretation they have in mind and because of the monitoring function that teachers naturally perform when they are in charge of a discussion.

Tharp and Gailimore (1989) use the terms *responsive teaching and instructional conversations* to contrast effective teacher-student dialogues with such recitations. In responsive teaching, teachers plan instruction by anticipating a range of student responses in addition to thinking about their own interpretations. They then use student input into discussions and student text interpretations to move the discussion to higher levels. Teachers might still nominate topics and opinions for group consideration, but student input drives the discussion forward.

Changing the pattern of classroom discussions to allow more student input and control is no easy task. Alvermann and Hayes (1989), for example, found that it was much easier for teachers to change the *level* of questions they asked (for example, move to more inferential, evaluative, and critical thinking questions) than it was for them to change the basic *structure* or pattern of interactions in classroom discussions. Teachers suggested two main reasons for the persistence of the recitation format in their classrooms: maintaining control and ensuring coverage of important information and canonical interpretations.

2. *Accepting personal interpretations and reactions.*
    A broader definition of comprehension, one that includes the possibility of multiple interpretations and the importance of readers' responses to their reading, is behind many of the changes proposed for discussions in recent years. This respect for individual response and interpretation has been nurtured by the growth in popularity of the response to literature tradition (Beach and Hynds 1991). In particular, Rosenblatt's (1978) distinction between *efferent reading*—that from which a reader gets information or basic meaning—*and aesthetic reading*—the actual lived-through experience of reading and responding personally to a text—has allowed us to treat reading experiences differentially. Recently, the process of allowing students to build, express, and defend their own interpretations has become a *revalued* goal of text discussions.

    Eeds and her colleagues use the term *grand conversations* to describe literature discussions in which the teacher's role is to be a coequal in the discussion, instead of the leader of a *gentle inquisition* (Eeds and Wells 1989, Peterson and Eeds 1990). In this role, the teacher can capitalize on teachable moments, help clarify confusions, keep track of students' ideas, and suggest ideas for consideration without insisting on a unitary interpretation of the text.

    A typical concern about such discussions is that students might spend a lot of time talking about personal reactions but come away from the discussion not really "understanding" what they have read or not having taken the opportunity to discuss important text features. In analyses of such discussions of literary texts, however, Eeds and Wells (1989) and others (Raphael et al. 1992, Rogers 1991) have found that students engage in a variety of activities important to understanding:

    - using the whole range of responses, from literal to critical and evaluative;

    - clarifying the basic meaning of the text when there are confusions or disagreements; and

    - using the opinions of others—including classmates, teacher, and published critics—to help clarify their thinking about a text.

In some of these studies, writing also has been an important avenue for students to understand text: (a) by documenting their independent thinking before group discussion and, (b) by synthesizing information and figuring out how their thinking has changed after discussion.

3. *Embedding strategy instruction in text reading.*
   Even in teacher-student discussions focused around a shared understanding of important text information, new ideas are emerging about how to build this shared understanding in a way that will teach students something about comprehension as well as text information. For example, in *situated cognition.* (Brown et al. 1989), learning about comprehension strategies is embedded in discussions about texts. The cognitive activities students engage in are much like the ones that have been the focus of research about explicit instruction in comprehension strategies, such as summarizing and getting the main idea. The difference is that the focus is on learning authentic information in the texts—for example, discovering how photosynthesis works by reading a chapter about it—with comprehension strategy learning as a secondary outcome of repeated engagement in such discussions about many different texts. The belief is that students will internalize effective comprehension strategies through repeated situations in which they read and discuss whole texts with a teacher and peers.

A Call for Multiple Approaches

When we teach courses about reading instruction for preservice and inservice teachers, we sometimes hear the complaint that researchers seem to pit approaches against one another instead of exploring how a particular innovation might operate as part of a total program. This is a legitimate concern, because if innovations are viewed as dichotomous, children may end up with instruction that is deficient in some areas.

Anything less than a well-rounded instructional program is a form of discrimination against children who have difficulty with reading. Delpit (1988), for example, asserts that children from non-mainstream backgrounds deserve to be taught directly what their mainstream teachers want them to do in order to read and comprehend texts. Slavin (1987) contends that an important outcome of cooperative learning is that it eliminates the segregation along racial and socioeconomic lines that often accompanies ability grouping. And Stanovich (1986) argues that if less able readers continually are denied opportunities to read actual texts, they will inevitably fall further and further behind—the rich will get richer and the poor will get poorer. Clearly, then, multiple approaches to comprehension improvement are in order. To use the recent language of the standards debate, a full portfolio of teacher strategies designed to promote a full portfolio of student strategies could be construed as essential in meeting opportunity-to-learn standards.

We see no reason why all four of the components described here—ample time for actual text reading, teacher-directed comprehension strategy instruction, opportunities for peer and collaborative learning, and time to talk about what has been read—should not complement one another in the same classroom. Nor do we see why the appropriateness of any component would depend on whether the primary reading material is children's literature or basal readers. We do believe, however, that if our ultimate goal is to develop independent, motivated comprehenders who choose to read, then a substantial part of children's reading instructional time each day must be devoted to self-selected materials that are within the students' reach. It is through such reading that children can experience the successful comprehension, learning, independence, and interest that will motivate future reading.

References

Allington, R. L. (1983a). "Fluency: The Neglected Reading Goal." *The Reading Teacher* 36: 556-561.

Allington, R. L. (1983b). "The Reading Instruction Provided Readers of Differing Reading Abilities." *Elementary School Journal* 83: 548-559.

Alvermann, D. E., and D. A. Hayes. (1989). "Classroom Discussion of Content Area Reading Assignments: An Intervention Study." *Reading Research Quarterly* 24: 305-335.

Anderson, R. C., E. H. Hiebert, J.A. Scott, and I.A.G. Wilkinson. (1985). *Becoming a Nation of Readers.* Washington, D. C.: National Institute of Education.

Anderson, R. C., L. Shirey, P. T. Wilson, and L. G. Fielding. (1987). "Interestingness of Children's Reading Material." In *Aptitude, Learning, and Instruction. Vol 3: Conative and Affective Process Analyses,* edited by R. Snow and M. Farr. Hillsdale, N. J.: Erlbaum.

Anderson, R. C., P. T. Wilson, and L. G. Fielding. (1988). "Growth in Reading and How Children Spend Their Time Outside of School." *Reading Research Quarterly* 23: 285-303.

Armbruster, B. B., T. H. Anderson, and J. Ostertag. (1987). "Does Text Structure/Summarization Instruction Facilitate Learning From Expository Text?" *Reading Research Quarterly* 22:331-346.

Atwell, N. (1987). *In the Middle.* Montclair, N. J.: Boynton/Cook.

Baumann, J. F. (1984). "Effectiveness of a Direct Instruction Paradigm for Teaching Main Idea Comprehension." *Reading Research Quarterly* 20: 93-108.

Beach, R., and S. Hynds. (1991). "Research on Response to Literature." In *Handbook of Reading Research: Vol II,* edited by . Barr, M. Kamil, P. Mosenthal, and P.D. Pearson. New York: Longman.

Beck, I.L., R. C. Omanson, and M. G. McKeown. (1982). "An Instructional Redesign of Reading Lessons: Effects on Comprehension." *Reading Research Quarterly* 17:462-481.

Brown, J. S., A. Collins, and P. Duguid. (1989). "Situated Cognition and the Culture of Learning." *Educational Researcher* 18, 1: 3242.

Cazden, C. (1986). "Classroom Discourse." In *Handbook of Research on Teaching,* 3rd ed., edited by M. C. Wittrock. New York: Macmillan.

Delpit, L. (1988). "The Silenced Dialogue:Power and Pedagogy in Educating Other People's Children." *Harvard Educational Review* 58, 3: 280-298.

Dowhower, S. L. (1987). "Effects of Repeated Reading on Second-Grade Transitional Readers' Fluency and Comprehension." *Reading Research Quarterly* 22: 389–406.

Duffy, G., L. Roehler, and B. Hermann. (1988). "Modeling Mental Processes Helps Poor Readers Become Strategic Readers." *The Reading Teacher* 41: 762-767.

Durkin, D. (1978-1979). "What Classroom Observations Reveal About Reading Comprehension Instruction." *Reading Research Quarterly* 15: 481-533. Eeds, M., and D. Wells. (1989). "Grand Conversations: An Exploration of Meaning Construction in Literature Study Groups." *Research in the Teaching of English* 23: 4-29. Elley, W. B. (1989). "Vocabulary Acquisition from Listening to Stories." *Reading Research Quarterly* 24: 174-187.

Fitzgerald, J., and D. L. Spiegel. (1983). "Enhancing Children's Reading Comprehension Through Instruction in Narrative Structure." *Journal of Reading Behavior* 15, 2: 1-17.

Hansen, J. (1987). *When Writers Read.* Portsmouth, N. H.: Heinemann.

Hansen, J., and P. D. Pearson. (1983). "An Instructional Study: Improving Inferential Comprehension of Good and Poor Fourth-Grade Readers." *Journal of Educational Psychology* 75: 821-829.

Johnson, D., and R. Johnson. (1985). "The Internal Dynamics of Cooperative Learning Groups." In *Learning to Cooperate, Cooperating to Learn,* edited by R. Slavin, S. Sharon, S. Kagan, R. Hertz-Lazarowitz, C. Webb, and R. Schmuck. New York: Plenum Press.

Koskinen, P., and I. Blum. (1986). "Paired Repeated Reading: A Classroom Strategy for Developing Fluent Reading." *The Reading Teacher* 40: 70-75.

Labbo, L., and W. Teale. (1990). "Cross-Age Reading: A Strategy for Helping Poor Readers." *The Reading Teacher* 43: 362-369.

Leinhardt, G., N. Zigmond, and W. Cooley. (1981). "Reading Instruction and Its Effects." *American Educational Research Journal* 18: 343-361.

Manning, G. L., and M. Manning. (1984). "What Models of Recreational Reading Make a Difference?" *Reading World* 23: 375-380.

Meloth, M. (1991). "Enhancing Literacy Through Cooperative Learning." In *Literacy for a Diverse Society: Perspectives, Practices, and Policies,* edited by E. Hiebert. New York: Teachers College Press.

Nagy, W. E., R. C. Anderson, and P. A. Herman. (1987). "Learning Word Meanings from Context During Normal Reading." *American Educational Research Journal* 24: 237-270.

Ogle, D. (1986). "K-W-L: A Teaching Model That Develops Active Reading of Expository Text." *The Reading Teacher* 39: 564-570.

Palincsar, A. S., A. L. Brown, and S. M. Martin. (1987). "Peer Interaction in Reading Comprehension Instruction." *Educational Psychologist* 22: 231-253.

Paris, S. G., V. A. Wasik, and J. C. Turner. (1991). "The Development of Strategic Readers." In *Handbook of Reading Research: Vol. II,* edited by R. Barr, M. Kamil, P. Mosenthal, and P. D. Pearson New York: Longman.

Pearson, P. D., and J. A. Dole. (1987). "Explicit Comprehension Instruction: A Review of Research and a New Conceptualization of Instruction." *Elementary School Journal* 88, 2: 151-165.

Pearson, P. D., and L. G. Fielding. (1991). "Comprehension Instruction." In *Handbook of Reading Research: Vol. II,* edited by R. Barr, M. Kamil, P. Mosenthal, and P. D. Pearson. New York: Longman.

Peterson, R., and M. Eeds. (1990). *Grand Conversations: Literature Groups in Action.* New York: Scholastic.

Raphael, T., S. McMahon, V. Goatley, J.Bentley, F. Boyd, L. Pardo, and D. Woodman. (1992). "Research Directions: Literature and Discussion in the Reading Program." *Language Arts* 69: 54-61.

Raphael, T. E., and P. D. Pearson. (1985). "Increasing Students' Awareness of Sources of Information for Answering Questions." *American Educational Research Journal* 22: 217-236.

Rogers, T. (1991). "Students as Literary Critics: The Interpretive Experiences, Beliefs, and Processes of Ninth-Grade Students." *Journal of Reading Behavior* 23: 391–423.

Rosenblatt, L. (1978). *The Reader, the Text, the Poem: The Transactional Theory of a Literary Work.* Carbondale, Ill.: Southern Illinois University Press.

Slavin, R. E. (1987). "Cooperative Learning and the Cooperative School." *Educational Leadership* 45, 3: 7-13.

Stallman, A. (1991). "Learning Vocabulary from Context: Effects of Focusing Attention on Individual Words During Reading." Doctoral diss., University of Illinois, Urbana-Champaign.

Stanovich, K. (1986). "Matthew Effects in Reading: Some Consequences of Individual Differences in the Acquisition of Literacy." *Reading Research Quarterly* 21: 360-407.

Stevens, R., N. Madden, R. Slavin, and A. Farnish. (1987). "Cooperative Integrated Reading and Composition: Two Field Experiments." *Reading Research Quarterly* 22: 433-454.

Tharp, R. G., and R. Gallimore. (1989), *Rousing Minds to Life: Teaching, Learning and Schooling in Social Context.* New York: Cambridge University Press.

Modifying Comprehension Assessment Measures

- Teachers can write one or two purpose-setting questions for each reading comprehension passage. The intent of such questions is to help students activate appropriate schemata for comprehending the passage (Rowe & Rayford, 1987). Purpose-setting questions that relate to students' experiential/conceptual backgrounds and are rich in information will better enable readers to activate appropriate schemata.

- Teachers can write three or four summaries for each comprehension passage and have students select the one that they think best describes the selection (Valencia & Pearson, 1987). Teachers should discuss with students why they selected a particular summary. Students can also be encouraged to elaborate on the summaries, providing information they feel would be helpful for telling someone else about the passage.

- Teachers can have students rate their familiarity with each passage after they have read it and answered the accompanying questions. A rating scale such as **I knew a lot**, **I knew something**, **I knew very little** for each passage can be developed. Students' comprehension for familiar topics versus unfamiliar topics can then be compared to ascertain their comprehension abilities in relation to their experiential/conceptual backgrounds. Teachers can also have students rate the difficulty of each passage in terms of word identification, vocabulary, and language structure to gain insights into how these influenced their comprehension. For example, teachers can ask their students if a selection was hard to read because the words were difficult to identify, the meanings of the words were difficult to figure out, or the sentences and how they were arranged made the passage difficult to read.

- In a small group or with the whole class, students can discuss with the teacher which multiple-choice answers for each question are either close to being correct, not close to being correct, or are correct. This will provide information about how students activate their experiential/conceptual backgrounds in relation to their choices identified for each question. Students can be encouraged to discuss why each possible answer for a question is correct or partially correct. Students can also be directed to discuss with the teacher what information would have to be included in the passage for each of the possible answers to be correct. This will provide information about the students' abilities to elaborate on text information by using inferences.

- Teachers can write additional questions for each comprehension passage and have students select those they think will help a classmate best understand the important ideas in the passage (Valencia & Pearson, 1987).

- Teachers can rewrite test questions to include some that are evaluative in nature. These can be administered to students and then students can discuss in groups their responses and how they arrived at their responses.

- Teachers can list information that might or might not be found in each comprehension test passage. Prior to reading the passage, students can predict whether or not the listed information would, would not, or would possibly appear in the passage. Their predictions will give the teacher insights into students' prior knowledge before reading the selection (Valencia & Pearson, 1987).

- Students can be directed to examine the titles of passages while the teacher assists them with predicting what kinds of information they are likely to find in each passage and with identifying questions they would like to answer about the content. This will help students establish purposes for reading.